מסורה

ArtScroll Mesorah Series®

Rabbi Nosson Scherman / Rabbi Meir Zlotowitz

eral Editors

⮹ The Seif Edition of the Transliterated Haggadah

It is a welcome phenomenon in our time that countless people with limited Jewish education are becoming increasingly interested in learning about and participating in their Jewish heritage. Thanks to **Herbert and Harriet Seif**, even those of them who cannot as yet read Hebrew can now feel perfectly comfortable in the synagogue or at a traditional Seder table, where the language of the service is Hebrew.

In this Haggadah and in the other liturgical works in the Seif Series, each Hebrew phrase is transliterated, so that the participant sees the Hebrew spelled with English letters. Thus, the reader can "hear" the words as they are pronounced and even read them himself. As an added service, the English translation appears on the line below. The finished product is like a personal invitation to join, and understand, the service.

Other works in the Seif Interlinear Series include:
- The Transliterated Weekday Siddur
- The Transliterated Sabbath and Festival Siddur
- The Transliterated Rosh Hashanah Machzor
- The Transliterated Yom Kippur Machzor

A PROJECT OF THE

Mesorah Heritage Foundation

הגדה של פסח

Haggadah

Published by

Mesorah Publications, ltd

THE SEIF EDITION

Transliterated Linear

Translation and Introduction by
Rabbi Nosson Scherman

Notes by
Rabbi Avie Gold

Designed and Produced by
Rabbi Sheah Brander

FIRST EDITION
First Impression . . . March 2004
Second Impression . . . February 2006
Third Impression . . . February 2009
Fourth Impression . . . February 2010

THE ARTSCROLL SERIES ®
THE SEIF EDITION
TRANSLITERATED LINEAR HAGGADAH

© *Copyright 2004 by* MESORAH PUBLICATIONS, Ltd.
4401 Second Avenue / Brooklyn, N.Y. 11232 / (718) 921-9000 / www.artscroll.com

Printed in Canada
ISBN 10: 1-4226-0967-7 / ISBN 13: 978-1-4226-0967-5 (h/c)
ISBN 10: 1-57819-316-8 / ISBN 13: 978-1-57819-316-5 (p/b)

Typography by CompuScribe at ArtScroll Studios, Ltd.

This volume is lovingly dedicated
to our children and grandson

**Yehuda and Orit Seif
Abie, Izzy, and Uriel**

Our goal for our children has always been
that they live up to the maximum of their potential.
Yehudah and Orit have more than satisfied
our greatest expectations.

In Torah learning, in general education,
and in their sterling character,
they are role models of young people
who add luster to our heritage and pride to their families.
What is more, they are conveying the depth and beauty
of the Torah to college students, and creating a thirst
for knowledge and observance of mitzvos.

It is fitting that we honor their achievement
through this transliterated Haggadah.
It, like they, connects the glory of the past
to the promise of the future.
May Yehuda and Orit always be blessed
with the ability to carry out their noble ambitions
for the sake of our people.

Harriet and Herbert Seif

⋐§ Guide to Reading the Transliteration

Consonants are read as they sound in English, except for "ch" (ח,כ,ך) which is pronounced as in *challah*.

The "silent" Hebrew letters — א and ע, whenever they appear, and ה, when it appears at the end of a word — are not represented. Although the letter ה is not usually pronounced when it appears at the end of a word, there are exceptions to the rule. These exceptions are indicated in Hebrew by a dot inside the letter — הּ. In transliteration the ה appears as a final h and is preceded by a vowel.

A consonant is usually pronounced together with the vowel following it. Thus, הַמֶּלֶךְ, "hamelech," is pronounced "ha-me-lech," and not "ham-el-ech." Hyphens are used to indicate exceptions to this rule.

When two consonants appear in tandem (except for those that are pronounced as a single sound, such as, ch, sh, tz), the first ends a syllable and the second begins a new syllable. Thus, וּבְנֵה, "uvnay," is pronounced "uv-nay"; אֶקְרָא, "ekro," is pronounced "ek-ro" not "e-kro."

Vowels are pronounced as follows:

a	אַ	as in	**hurrah**
o	אָ	as in	**often**
ō	א or אוֹ	as in	**post**
ay	אֵ or אֵי	as in	**pay**
e	אֶ	as in	**leg**
i	א or אִי	as in	**machine**
u	אֻ or אוּ	as in	**lunar**
oy	אֹי	as in	**boy**
ai	אַי	as in	**aisle**

The sounded *sh'va* (בְּ) is represented by an apostrophe (b') and is pronounced similarly to the indistinct **a** in **ago**.

Hyphens are used to separate syllables that might otherwise be slurred into each other (e.g., מֵעַתָּה is transliterated "may-ato" not "ma-yato").

Capital letters are not used in Hebrew. However, for the convenience of the reader, the transliteration uses a capital letter to indicate the beginning of a verse or a sentence. Additionally, capitals are used to indicate Divine Names which may not be pronounced except as part of a Scriptural verse or within a prayer.

Note: Phrases in the transliteration or instructions that are followed by an asterisk (*) are discussed in the commentary below, usually on the same page, but sometimes on the facing or following pages.

The mark ❖ indicates the point at which the *chazzan* begins reciting aloud.

❧ Table of Contents

✑ The Seder /
A Celebration of Freedom and Family

The family aspect of the Seder is an integral part of the observance, for the Torah speaks frequently of the responsibility of parents to teach their children about the Exodus.

This is a night when bonds are forged between parent and child, when the chain of generations is strengthened and new links are added.

Every era has its Egypt, its own brand of slavery and temptation that inhibits the development of Israel. And to every generation, the Seder says that this night is different.

Hardly a ceremony in Jewish life is more familiar and more widely observed than the Passover Seder. For countless grandparents and parents, it represents an "ingathering of exiles" of sorts, as children converge from far and wide to celebrate the Seder together. Indeed, the family aspect of the Seder is an integral part of the observance, for the Torah speaks frequently of the responsibility of parents to teach their children about the Exodus.

Of no other commandment does the Torah speak about children's questions and parents' answers. So when the youngest member of the household is coaxed, bribed and encouraged to stand before Zaidy or Daddy and say the *Mah Nishtanah,* the Four Questions, the heartwarming ritual is truly an essential part of the Seder — for this is a night when bonds are forged between parent and child, when the chain of generations is strengthened and new links are added. It is a night when, as we say in the Haggadah, every Jew should regard himself as though *he* were freed from Egyptian slavery, and began the march from the land of his bondage toward Sinai, where Israel would receive the gift of the Ten Commandments.

So important is that aspect of the interaction between parent and child that the Sages instituted some Seder customs primarily to stimulate the curiosity of youngsters. Let them ask. Let their parents answer. Let everyone inquire, think, delve, innovate, find ways to relate the adventure of old to the challenges of today. For the Seder and its narrative speak to every generation. Every era has its Egypt, its own brand of slavery and temptation that inhibits the development of Israel. And to every generation, the Seder says that this night *is* different, because it brings home lessons that can easily be drowned in the constant activity of daily life.

The Talmud lays down the dictum that our narrative of freedom must begin with the tale of our degradation, for it is only when someone recalls how bad things *were* that he can realize how good things *are*. The Haggadah's narrative of the torturous slavery of Egypt is understandable — that was bondage in its most literal sense. Surely freedom must have been sweet to the Jew whose back still smarted from the scars of the taskmaster's whip, to the mother whose child had been bricked into a pyramid or drowned in the Nile.

Surely freedom must have been sweet to the Jew whose back still smarted from the scars of the taskmaster's whip.

But the Haggadah contains a second narrative of degradation and our escape from it: *Originally our ancestors were idol worshipers, but now the Omnipresent has brought us near to His service.* There is another slavery, another degradation, one that is *not* to masters holding whips, enforcing production quotas, murdering children, separating families. Idolatry, too, is a form of enslavement, for when people choose idols that suit their own desires and concerns, they are truly slaves — to their own passions. Our ancestors were pagans. As pagans they were spiritually flawed and they would have passed on their spiritual blemish to their posterity, had not Israel been liberated from this slavery to codes of man's own creation.

Idolatry, too, is a form of enslavement, for when people choose idols that suit their own desires and concerns, they are truly slaves — to their own passions.

So the Exodus represented a twofold liberation: from physical enslavement and from spiritual degradation. The nation as a whole was cleansed of both blemishes. On the night of Passover it came to acknowledge no master but God and it began the trek to the wilderness where it would stand at Sinai and declare its willingness to accept the privilege of bearing God's message of truth and morality.

Are the enslavement of Pharaoh and the idolatry of Terach behind us? The Seder is not only a celebration of past liberation but also a challenge to retain it.

Are the enslavement of Pharaoh and the idolatry of Terach behind us? Hardly. History books and newspapers alike illustrate all too vividly that physical independence is easily lost and moral freedom easily subverted. The Seder is not only a celebration of past liberation but also a challenge to retain it. That is why we declare the responsibility of every Jewish man, woman and child to regard himself or herself as one of those hundreds of thousands who departed Egypt for a better life and a greater responsibility. Only by understanding the past and identifying with it can we deal intelligently with the future. Terach tried to impose idolatry on his children — so he was our enemy. Laban tried to wean his grandchildren, the first totally Jewish family, away from the faith of Abraham, Isaac and Jacob — so he was our enemy. Pharaoh tried to destroy Jewish nationhood and tried to assimilate it into the Egyptian people — so he was our enemy. These were different kinds of challenges and one or the other is a mirror of virtually every danger — bitter or sweet — that has ever confronted Israel.

Therefore we gather our generations around the Seder table and transmit the message of Jewish history to our children. According to the Halachah, the Seder narrative must be understood; indeed, the great scholars of Jewish history made it a point to translate and simplify the Haggadah so that everyone at their tables could understand. As the Haggadah tells us, the greatest sages of their time gathered in Bnei Brak to discuss the redemption and its implications for them. And as the Haggadah tells us, the Seder night is the time to relate the narrative to our children — from the wisest to the simplest — encouraging them to ask, inquire, challenge, learn; for only by doing so can they become part of Jewish history and make it part of their own personal experience and perspective of the world.

According to Halachah, the Seder night is the time to relate the narrative to our children, encouraging them to ask, inquire, challenge, learn.

The Seder is a celebration of history — the past *and* the future. Though we Jews always learn from our past, we simultaneously look ahead to a future of spiritual perfection. This is symbolized by the Hallel prayer of the Seder. The first two chapters of Hallel refer to the miracles of the Exodus; they are recited just before the Seder feast. Following the festive meal with its many *mitzvos,* we continue with the rest of Hallel, the ecstatic songs of hope and prayer that allude to the prophetic visions of plowshares taking the place of swords and of Jerusalem displacing the martial capitals of the world.

Let us hear its message of the past and let it teach us how to order our present that we may build a better future.

Let us gather up our children and ourselves, to begin the Seder. Let us hear its message of the past and let it teach us how to order our present that we may build a better future.

ও Preparing for Passover

❑ בדיקת חמץ /
The Search for Chametz

Aside from the commandment to eat matzah all of Passover and the special observances of the Seder nights, the best-known feature of the festival is the requirement not to eat, or even to own, chametz all during the festival. For many Jews, one of the most vivid memories of their childhood is the seemingly endless cleaning and scrubbing of their homes during the weeks and days before Passover.

Although no household can be thoroughly cleaned in only a short while, the Talmudic Sages ordained that a search for chametz be made in every home and business on one night of the year.

The search begins upon nightfall of the fourteenth day of Nissan, the evening before Passover. The purpose of the commandment is the removal of all chametz, and it requires a formal inspection of all areas where chametz may have been brought during the course of the year — despite the fact that a thorough cleaning was made before Passover. The search should be made by candlelight, and one may not speak until it is completed — except to give instructions or make inquiries directly relating to the search.

In years when Passover begins on Saturday night, the inspection is not conducted on the evening before Passover, for this would result in a desecration of the Sabbath. Instead, it is made on Thursday night and the chametz is burned Friday morning.

A widespread custom calls for the distribution of ten pieces of chametz through the house before the search (by someone other than the person conducting the search). Of course, care should be taken that the pieces do not leave crumbs, thereby defeating the purpose of the search.

Any chametz intended for that evening's supper or the next morning's breakfast must be set aside carefully. After one finishes eating, leftover chametz should be placed with whatever chametz may have been found in the evening. It will be burned the morning before Passover (except when Passover begins on Saturday night, in which case the chametz is burned Friday morning).

■ A Jew may not even own chametz/leaven on Pesach.
We therefore both rid and then annul all chametz from our possession.

ON THE NIGHT OF 14 NISSAN, THE NIGHT BEFORE THE PESACH SEDER, THE SEARCH FOR
CHAMETZ (LEAVEN) IS MADE. IT SHOULD BE DONE WITH A CANDLE AS SOON AS POSSIBLE
AFTER NIGHTFALL. [WHEN THE FIRST SEDER IS ON SATURDAY NIGHT, THE SEARCH IS CON-
DUCTED ON THURSDAY NIGHT (13 NISSAN).] BEFORE THE SEARCH IS BEGUN, THE FOLLOWING
BLESSING IS RECITED. IF SEVERAL PEOPLE ASSIST IN THE SEARCH, ONLY ONE RECITES THE
BLESSING FOR ALL.

BORUCH ato Adōnoy   בָּרוּךְ אַתָּה יהוה

Blessed are You, HASHEM,

Elōhaynu melech ho-ōlom,   אֱלֹהֵינוּ מֶלֶךְ הָעוֹלָם,

our God, King of the universe,

asher kid'shonu b'mitzvōsov,   אֲשֶׁר קִדְּשָׁנוּ בְּמִצְוֹתָיו,

Who has sanctified us with His commandments

v'tzivonu al bi-ur chomaytz.   וְצִוָּנוּ עַל בִּעוּר חָמֵץ.

and has commanded us concerning the removal of chametz.

ALL PRESENT RESPOND: Omayn — אָמֵן

AFTER THE SEARCH, THE *CHAMETZ* IS WRAPPED AND PUT ASIDE IN A SAFE PLACE
TO BE BURNED IN THE MORNING. THEN THE FOLLOWING DECLARATION IS MADE.

■ It is essential that all chametz be declared ownerless so that one not be in possession of chametz without knowing it. The evening declaration carefully omits any
chametz that one wishes to retain for the next day's breakfast, the chametz that
will be burned the next morning and the chametz that will be sold to a non-Jew in
the morning.

UPON COMPLETION OF THE CHAMETZ SEARCH, THE CHAMETZ IS WRAPPED WELL AND SET
ASIDE TO BE BURNED THE NEXT MORNING, AND THE FOLLOWING DECLARATION IS MADE. ANY
CHAMETZ THAT WILL BE USED FOR THAT EVENING'S SUPPER OR THE NEXT DAY'S BREAKFAST OR
FOR ANY OTHER PURPOSE PRIOR TO THE FINAL REMOVAL OF CHAMETZ THE NEXT MORNING
IS NOT INCLUDED IN THIS DECLARATION.
THIS IS A LEGAL DECLARATION, NOT A PRAYER; THEREFORE IT MUST BE UNDERSTOOD. IF ONE
DOES NOT UNDERSTAND THE ARAMAIC, HE SHOULD RECITE IT IN A LANGUAGE HE UNDER-
STANDS. PREFERABLY, IT SHOULD BE RECITED BY ALL MEMBERS OF THE FAMILY.

KOL CHAMIRO vachami-o   כָּל חֲמִירָא וַחֲמִיעָא

Any chametz or leaven

d'iko virshusi   דְּאִכָּא בִרְשׁוּתִי,

that is in my possession,

d'lo chazitayh (d'lo chamitayh)   דְּלָא חֲזִתֵּה (דְּלָא חֲמִתֵּה)

which I have not recognized (which I have not seen),

ud-lo vi-artayh   וּדְלָא בְעַרְתֵּהּ

have not removed

ud-lo y'dano layh,   וּדְלָא יְדַעְנָא לֵיהּ,

and do not know about,

libotayl v'lehevay hefkayr   לִבָּטֵל וְלֶהֱוֵי הֶפְקֵר

should be annulled and become ownerless,

k'afro d'ar-o.   כְּעַפְרָא דְאַרְעָא.

like dust of the earth.

❑ בִּיעוּר חָמֵץ /
Burning the Chametz

THE FOLLOWING DECLARATION, WHICH INCLUDES ALL CHAMETZ WITHOUT EXCEPTION,
IS TO BE MADE AFTER THE BURNING OF LEFTOVER CHAMETZ. IT SHOULD BE RECITED IN
A LANGUAGE WHICH ONE UNDERSTANDS. WHEN PASSOVER BEGINS ON SATURDAY NIGHT,
THIS DECLARATION IS MADE ON SATURDAY MORNING. ANY CHAMETZ REMAINING FROM
THE SATURDAY-MORNING MEAL IS FLUSHED DOWN THE DRAIN BEFORE THE DECLARATION
IS MADE.

KOL CHAMIRO vachami-o   **כָּל חֲמִירָא** וַחֲמִיעָא

Any chametz or leaven

d'iko virshusi,   דְּאִכָּא בִרְשׁוּתִי,

that is in my possession,

da-chazitayh ud-lo chazitayh,   דַּחֲזִתֵּהּ וּדְלָא חֲזִתֵּהּ,

whether I have recognized it or not,

(da-chamitayh ud-lo chamitayh),   (דַּחֲמִתֵּהּ וּדְלָא חֲמִתֵּהּ),

(whether I have seen it or not),

d'vi-artayh ud-lo vi-artayh,   דְּבְעַרְתֵּהּ וּדְלָא בְעַרְתֵּהּ,

whether I have removed it or not,

libotayl v'lehevay hefkayr   לִבָּטֵל וְלֶהֱוֵי הֶפְקֵר

should be annulled and become ownerless,

k'afro d'ar-o.   כְּעַפְרָא דְאַרְעָא.

like dust of the earth.

❑ עירוב תבשילין / Ayruv Tavshilin

IT IS FORBIDDEN TO PREPARE ON YOM TOV FOR THE NEXT DAY EVEN IF THAT DAY IS THE SABBATH.
IF, HOWEVER, SABBATH PREPARATIONS WERE STARTED BEFORE YOM TOV BEGAN, THEY MAY
BE CONTINUED ON YOM TOV. ERUV TAVSHILIN CONSTITUTES THIS PREPARATION. A MATZAH
AND ANY COOKED FOOD (SUCH AS FISH, MEAT, OR AN EGG) ARE SET ASIDE ON THE DAY BEFORE
YOM TOV TO BE USED ON THE SABBATH AND THE BLESSING IS RECITED FOLLOWED BY THE
DECLARATION [MADE IN A LANGUAGE UNDERSTOOD BY THE ONE MAKING THE ERUV].

IF THE FIRST DAYS OF PASSOVER FALL ON THURSDAY AND FRIDAY,
AN ERUV TAVSHILIN MUST BE MADE ON WEDNESDAY.

IN ERETZ YISRAEL, WHERE ONLY ONE DAY YOM TOV IS IN EFFECT, THE ERUV IS OMITTED.

THE ERUV-FOODS ARE HELD WHILE THE FOLLOWING BLESSING AND DECLARATION ARE RECITED:

BORUCH ato Adōnoy   בָּרוּךְ אַתָּה יהוה
Blessed are You, HASHEM,

Elōhaynu melech ho-ōlom,   אֱלֹהֵינוּ מֶלֶךְ הָעוֹלָם,
our God, King of the universe,

asher kid'shonu b'mitzvōsov,   אֲשֶׁר קִדְּשָׁנוּ בְּמִצְוֹתָיו,
Who has sanctified us with His commandments

v'tzivonu al mitzvas ayruv.   וְצִוָּנוּ עַל מִצְוַת עֵרוּב.
and has commanded us concerning the mitzvah of eruv.

ALL PRESENT RESPOND: Omayn — אָמֵן

BAHADAYN ayruvo   בַּהֲדֵין עֵרוּבָא
Through this eruv

y'hay shoray lono   יְהֵא שָׁרֵא לָנָא
may we be permitted

la-afu-yay ulva-shulay ul-atmunay   לַאֲפוּיֵי וּלְבַשׁוּלֵי וּלְאַטְמוּנֵי
to bake, cook, insulate,

ul-adlukay sh'rogo ul-sakono   וּלְאַדְלוּקֵי שְׁרָגָא וּלְתַקָּנָא
kindle flame, prepare

ulmebad kol tzorkono,   וּלְמֶעְבַּד כָּל צָרְכָּנָא,
and do anything necessary

mi-yōmo tovo l'shab'so   מִיּוֹמָא טָבָא לְשַׁבְּתָא
on the Festival for the sake of the Sabbath

[lono ul-chol yisro-ayl   [לָנָא וּלְכָל יִשְׂרָאֵל
hadorim bo-ir ha-zōs].   הַדָּרִים בָּעִיר הַזֹּאת].
[for ourselves and for all Jews who live in this city].

❑ הדלקת הנרות / ❑
Lighting the Candles

THE CANDLES ARE LIT AND THE FOLLOWING BLESSINGS ARE RECITED.
WHEN YOM TOV FALLS ON THE SABBATH, THE WORDS IN PARENTHESES ARE ADDED.

BORUCH ato Adōnoy   בָּרוּךְ אַתָּה יהוה

Blessed are You, HASHEM,

Elōhaynu melech ho-ōlom,   אֱלֹהֵינוּ מֶלֶךְ הָעוֹלָם,

our God, King of the universe,

asher kid'shonu b'mitzvōsov,   אֲשֶׁר קִדְּשָׁנוּ בְּמִצְוֹתָיו,

Who has sanctified us with His commandments,

v'tzivonu l'hadlik nayr shel   וְצִוָּנוּ לְהַדְלִיק נֵר שֶׁל

and has commanded us to kindle the light of

ON THE SABBATH ADD:

shabos v'shel   שַׁבָּת וְשֶׁל

the Sabbath and of

yōm tōv.   יוֹם טוֹב.

the Festival.

BORUCH ato Adōnoy   בָּרוּךְ אַתָּה יהוה

Blessed are You, HASHEM,

Elōhaynu melech ho-ōlom,   אֱלֹהֵינוּ מֶלֶךְ הָעוֹלָם,

our God, King of the universe,

shehecheyonu   שֶׁהֶחֱיָנוּ

Who has kept us alive,

v'kiy'manu v'higi-onu   וְקִיְּמָנוּ וְהִגִּיעָנוּ

sustained us and brought us

laz'man ha-ze.   לַזְּמַן הַזֶּה.

to this season.

The Seder

◈§ The Seder Plate

The Seder preparations should be made in time for the Seder to begin as soon as the synagogue services are finished. It should not begin before nightfall, however. Matzah, bitter herbs and several other items of symbolic significance are placed on the Seder plate in the arrangement shown below.

ג' מצות – 3 MATZOS

Matzah — *Three whole matzos are placed one atop the other, separated by a cloth or napkin. Matzah must be eaten three times during the Seder: by itself, with maror, and as the afikoman. Each time, the minimum portion of matzah for each person should have a volume equivalent to half an egg. Where many people are present, enough matzos should be available to enable each participant to receive a proper portion.*

Maror and **Chazeres** — *Bitter herbs are eaten twice during the Seder, once by themselves and a second time with matzah. Each time a minimum portion, equal to the volume of half an egg, should be eaten. The Talmud lists several vegetables that qualify as maror, two of which are put on the Seder plate in the places marked chazeres and maror. Most people use romaine lettuce (whole leaves or stalks) for chazeres, and horseradish (whole or grated) for maror, although either may be used for the mitzvah of eating maror later in the Seder.*

Charoses — *The bitter herbs are dipped into charoses (a mixture of grated apples, nuts, other fruit, cinnamon and other spices, mixed with red wine). The charoses has the appearance of mortar to symbolize the lot of the Hebrew slaves, whose lives were embittered by hard labor with brick and mortar.*

Z'roa *[Roasted Bone]* and **Beitzah** *[Roasted Egg]* — *On the eve of Passover in the Holy Temple in Jerusalem, two sacrifices were offered and their meat roasted and eaten at the Seder feast. To commemorate these two sacrifices we place a roasted bone (with some meat on it) and a roasted hard-boiled egg on the Seder plate.*

The egg, a symbol of mourning, is used in place of a second piece of meat as a reminder of our mourning at the destruction of the Temple — may it be rebuilt speedily in our day.

Karpas — *A vegetable (celery, parsley, boiled potato) other than bitter herbs completes the Seder plate. It will be dipped in salt water and eaten. (The salt water is not put on the Seder plate, but it, too, should be prepared beforehand, and placed near the Seder plate.)*

৵৪ The Order of the Seder

The Seder ritual contains fifteen observances, which have been summarized in the familiar rhyme **Kaddesh, Urechatz, Karpas, Yachatz** *and so on. Aside from its convenience as a memory device, the brief formula has been given various deeper interpretations over the years. Accordingly, many people recite the appropriate word from the rhyme before performing the mitzvah to which it applies —* קַדֵּשׁ, *Kaddesh, before Kiddush,* וּרְחַץ, *Urechatz, before washing the hands, and so on.*

kadaysh	**Sanctify** the day with the recitation of Kiddush.	קַדֵּשׁ
ur'chatz	**Wash** the hands before eating Karpas.	וּרְחַץ
karpas	Eat a **vegetable** dipped in salt water.	כַּרְפַּס
yachatz	**Break** the middle matzah. Put away larger half for Afikoman	יַחַץ
magid	**Narrate** the story of the Exodus from Egypt.	מַגִּיד
roch'tzo	**Wash** the hands prior to the meal.	רָחְצָה
mõtzi	Recite the blessing, **Who brings forth,** over matzah as a food.	מוֹצִיא
matzo	Recite the blessing over **Matzah.**	מַצָּה
morõr	Recite the blessing for the eating of the **bitter herbs.**	מָרוֹר
kõraych	Eat the **sandwich** of matzah and bitter herbs	כּוֹרֵךְ
shulchon õraych	The **table prepared** with the festive meal.	שֻׁלְחָן עוֹרֵךְ
tzofun	Eat the afikoman which had been **hidden** all during the Seder.	צָפוּן
boraych	Recite Bircas Hamazon, the **blessings** after the meal.	בָּרֵךְ
halayl	Recite the **Hallel** Psalms of praise.	הַלֵּל
nirtzo	Pray that God **accept** our observance and speedily send the Messiah.	נִרְצָה

קַדֵּשׁ / KADAYSH

■ The holiness of the day is proclaimed by the recitation of Kiddush.

KIDDUSH SHOULD BE RECITED AND THE SEDER BEGUN AS SOON AFTER SYNAGOGUE SERVICES AS POSSIBLE — HOWEVER, NOT BEFORE NIGHTFALL. EACH PARTICIPANT'S CUP SHOULD BE POURED BY SOMEONE ELSE TO SYMBOLIZE THE MAJESTY OF THE EVENING, AS THOUGH EACH PARTICIPANT HAD A SERVANT.

ON FRIDAY NIGHT BEGIN HERE:

■ Although the night's proceedings focus on the Exodus, the Sabbath Kiddush takes precedence for it is the more common occurrence, and it commemorates an earlier event, the Creation.

THESE FOUR WORDS ARE RECITED IN AN UNDERTONE:

(Va-y'hi erev vaihi vōker)   (וַיְהִי עֶרֶב וַיְהִי בֹקֶר)

(And there was evening and there was morning)

YŌM HA-SHISHI.   **יוֹם הַשִּׁשִּׁי.**

The sixth day.

Va-y'chulu ha-shoma-yim v'ho-oretz   וַיְכֻלּוּ הַשָּׁמַיִם וְהָאָרֶץ
v'chol tz'vo-om.   וְכָל צְבָאָם.

Thus were finished the heavens and the earth, and all their array.

Va-y'chal Elōhim ba-yōm hash'vi-i   וַיְכַל אֱלֹהִים בַּיּוֹם הַשְּׁבִיעִי

On the seventh day God completed

m'lachtō asher oso,   מְלַאכְתּוֹ אֲשֶׁר עָשָׂה,

His work which He had done,

va-yishbōs ba-yōm hash'vi-i   וַיִּשְׁבֹּת בַּיּוֹם הַשְּׁבִיעִי

and He abstained on the seventh day

mikol m'lachtō asher oso.   מִכָּל מְלַאכְתּוֹ אֲשֶׁר עָשָׂה.

from all His work which He had done.

Vai-vorech Elōhim es   וַיְבָרֶךְ אֱלֹהִים אֶת
yōm hash'vi-i vai-kadaysh ōsō,   יוֹם הַשְּׁבִיעִי וַיְקַדֵּשׁ אֹתוֹ,

God blessed the seventh day and sanctified it,

ki vō shovas mikol m'lachtō   כִּי בוֹ שָׁבַת מִכָּל מְלַאכְתּוֹ

because on it He had abstained from all His work

asher boro Elōhim la-asōs.   אֲשֶׁר בָּרָא אֱלֹהִים לַעֲשׂוֹת.

which God created to make.

קַדֵּשׁ וּרְחַץ כַּרְפַּס יַחַץ מַגִּיד רָחְצָה מוֹצִיא מַ
kadaysh ur'chatz karpas yachatz magid roch'tzo mōtzi ...tzo

ON ALL NIGHTS OTHER THAN FRIDAY, BEGIN HERE;
ON FRIDAY NIGHT (THE SABBATH) INCLUDE ALL SHADED PASSAGES.

■ God has sanctified us with His commandments, and we, in turn,
sanctify Time by our fulfillment of His will.

Savri moronon v'rabonon v'rabōsai:　　סַבְרִי מָרָנָן וְרַבָּנָן וְרַבּוֹתַי:

By your leave, my masters, rabbis and teachers:

BORUCH ato Adōnoy　　בָּרוּךְ אַתָּה יהוה

Blessed are You, HASHEM,

Elōhaynu melech ho-ōlom,　　אֱלֹהֵינוּ מֶלֶךְ הָעוֹלָם,

our God, King of the universe,

bōray p'ri hagofen.　　בּוֹרֵא פְּרִי הַגָּפֶן.

Who creates the fruit of the vine.

ALL PRESENT RESPOND: Omayn — אָמֵן

BORUCH ato Adōnoy　　בָּרוּךְ אַתָּה יהוה

Blessed are You, HASHEM,

Elōhaynu melech ho-ōlom,　　אֱלֹהֵינוּ מֶלֶךְ הָעוֹלָם,

our God, King of the universe,

asher bochar bonu mikol om　　אֲשֶׁר בָּחַר בָּנוּ מִכָּל עָם,

Who has chosen us from every people,

v'rōm'monu mikol loshōn,　　וְרוֹמְמָנוּ מִכָּל לָשׁוֹן,

exalted us above every tongue,

v'kid'shonu b'mitzvōsov.　　וְקִדְּשָׁנוּ בְּמִצְוֹתָיו.

and sanctified us with His commandments.

Vatiten lonu　　וַתִּתֶּן לָנוּ

　Adōnoy Elōhaynu b'ahavo　　יהוה אֱלֹהֵינוּ בְּאַהֲבָה

And You gave us, HASHEM, our God, with love

ON THE SABBATH ADD:

shabosōs limnucho u . . .　　. . . שַׁבָּתוֹת לִמְנוּחָה וּ

Sabbaths for rest, and

mō-adim l'simcho,　　מוֹעֲדִים לְשִׂמְחָה

appointed Festivals for gladness,

chagim uz-manim l'sosōn,　　חַגִּים וּזְמַנִּים לְשָׂשׂוֹן,

Festivals and times for joy,

 שלחן עורך צפון ברך הלל נרצה

niRtzo　halayl　BORaych　tzofun　shulchon ōRaych　kōRaych　moRo

ON THE SABBATH ADD:

es yōm ha-shabos ha-ze v'...   ...וְ אֶת יוֹם הַשַּׁבָּת הַזֶּה

this day of Sabbath and

es yōm chag hamatzōs ha-ze,   אֶת יוֹם חַג הַמַּצוֹת הַזֶּה,

this day of the Festival of Matzos,

z'man chayrusaynu,   זְמַן חֵרוּתֵנוּ,

the time of our freedom,

ON THE SABBATH ADD:

b'ahavo   בְּאַהֲבָה

with love,

mikro kōdesh,   מִקְרָא קֹדֶשׁ,

a holy convocation,

zaycher litzi-as mitzro-yim.   זֵכֶר לִיצִיאַת מִצְרָיִם.

a memorial of the Exodus from Egypt.

Ki vonu vocharto,   כִּי בָנוּ בָחַרְתָּ

For You have chosen us

v'ōsonu kidashto mikol ho-amim,   וְאוֹתָנוּ קִדַּשְׁתָּ מִכָּל הָעַמִּים,

and You have sanctified us above all the peoples,

ON THE SABBATH ADD:

v'shabos   וְשַׁבָּת

and the Sabbath

u-mō-aday kod-shecho   וּמוֹעֲדֵי קָדְשֶׁךָ

and Your holy Festivals

ON THE SABBATH ADD:

b'ahavo uvrotzōn   בְּאַהֲבָה וּבְרָצוֹן

in love and in favor

b'simcho uvsosōn hinchaltonu.   בְּשִׂמְחָה וּבְשָׂשׂוֹן הִנְחַלְתָּנוּ.

in gladness and in joy have You granted us as a heritage.

Boruch ato Adōnoy, m'kadaysh   בָּרוּךְ אַתָּה יהוה, מְקַדֵּשׁ

Blessed are You, HASHEM, Who sanctifies

ON THE SABBATH ADD:

hashabos v'...   ...הַשַּׁבָּת וְ

the Sabbath and

yisro-ayl v'haz'manim.   יִשְׂרָאֵל וְהַזְּמַנִּים.

Israel and the (festive) seasons.

ALL PRESENT RESPOND: Omayn — אָמֵן

ON NIGHTS OTHER THAN SATURDAY NIGHT, CONTINUE IN THE MIDDLE OF PAGE 28.

ON SATURDAY NIGHT, ADD THE FOLLOWING TWO PARAGRAPHS:
TWO CANDLES WITH ONLY THEIR FLAMES TOUCHING ARE HELD AND THE FOLLOWING
BLESSINGS ARE RECITED. AFTER THE FIRST BLESSING, HOLD THE FINGERS UP TO THE FLAMES
TO SEE THE REFLECTED LIGHT.

BORUCH ato Adōnoy   בָּרוּךְ אַתָּה יהוה
Blessed are You, HASHEM,

Elōhaynu melech ho-ōlom,   אֱלֹהֵינוּ מֶלֶךְ הָעוֹלָם,
our God, King of the universe,

bōray m'ōray ho-aysh.   בּוֹרֵא מְאוֹרֵי הָאֵשׁ.
Who creates the illumination of the fire.

ALL PRESENT RESPOND: Omayn — אָמֵן

BORUCH ato Adōnoy,   בָּרוּךְ אַתָּה יהוה
Blessed are You, HASHEM,

Elōhaynu melech ho-ōlom,   אֱלֹהֵינוּ מֶלֶךְ הָעוֹלָם,
our God, King of the universe,

hamavdil bayn kōdesh l'chōl,   הַמַּבְדִּיל בֵּין קֹדֶשׁ לְחוֹל,
Who distinguishes between sacred and secular,

bayn ōr l'chōshech,   בֵּין אוֹר לְחֹשֶׁךְ,
between light and darkness,

bayn yisro-ayl lo-amim,   בֵּין יִשְׂרָאֵל לָעַמִּים,
between Israel and the peoples,

bayn yōm hash'vi-i,   בֵּין יוֹם הַשְּׁבִיעִי
between the Seventh Day

l'shayshes y'may hama-ase,   לְשֵׁשֶׁת יְמֵי הַמַּעֲשֶׂה.
and the six days of labor.

bayn k'dushas shabos   בֵּין קְדֻשַּׁת שַׁבָּת
Between the sanctity of the Sabbath

likdushas yōm tōv hivdalto,   לִקְדֻשַּׁת יוֹם טוֹב הִבְדַּלְתָּ,
and the sanctity of the holidays You have distinguished,

v'es yōm hash'vi-i   וְאֶת יוֹם הַשְּׁבִיעִי
and the Seventh Day,

mi-shayshes y'may hama-ase   מִשֵּׁשֶׁת יְמֵי הַמַּעֲשֶׂה
     kidashto,   קִדַּשְׁתָּ,
from among the six days of labor You have sanctified.

nirtzo   halayl   Boraych   tzofun   shulchon ōraych   kōraych   morō

hivdalto v'kidashto הִבְדַּלְתָּ וְקִדַּשְׁתָּ
You have distinguished and You have sanctified

es am'cho yisro-ayl אֶת עַמְּךָ יִשְׂרָאֵל
Your people Israel

bikdushosecho. בִּקְדֻשָּׁתֶךָ.
with Your holiness.

Boruch ato Adōnoy בָּרוּךְ אַתָּה יהוה,
Blessed are You, HASHEM,

hamavdil הַמַּבְדִּיל
Who distinguishes

bayn kōdesh l'kōdesh. בֵּין קֹדֶשׁ לְקֹדֶשׁ.
between holiness and holiness.

ALL PRESENT RESPOND: Omayn — אָמֵן

ON ALL NIGHTS CONTINUE HERE:

BORUCH ato Adōnoy **בָּרוּךְ** אַתָּה יהוה
Blessed are You, HASHEM,

Elōhaynu melech ho-ōlom, אֱלֹהֵינוּ מֶלֶךְ הָעוֹלָם,
our God, King of the universe,

shehecheyonu v'ki-y'monu שֶׁהֶחֱיָנוּ וְקִיְּמָנוּ
Who has kept us alive, sustained us,

v'higi-onu laz'man ha-ze. וְהִגִּיעָנוּ לַזְּמַן הַזֶּה.
and brought us to this season.

ALL PRESENT RESPOND: Omayn — אָמֵן

THE WINE SHOULD BE DRUNK WITHOUT DELAY WHILE RECLINING ON THE LEFT SIDE.
IT IS PREFERABLE TO DRINK THE ENTIRE CUP, BUT AT THE VERY LEAST,
MOST OF THE CUP SHOULD BE DRAINED.

וּרְחַץ / UR'CHATZ

WASH THE HANDS. THE HEAD OF THE HOUSEHOLD — ACCORDING TO MANY OPINIONS, ALL PARTICIPANTS IN THE SEDER — WASHES HIS HANDS AS IF TO EAT BREAD, [POURING WATER FROM A CUP, TWICE ON THE RIGHT HAND AND TWICE ON THE LEFT] BUT WITHOUT RECITING A BLESSING.

קַדֵּשׁ וּרְחַץ כַּרְפַּס יַחַץ מַגִּיד רָחְצָה מוֹצִיא מַצָּ
atzo   mōtzi   Roch'tzo   magid   yachatz   karpas   ur'chatz   kaoaysh

כַּרְפַּס / KARPAS

EAT KARPAS. ALL PARTICIPANTS TAKE A VEGETABLE OTHER THAN MAROR AND DIP IT INTO SALT-WATER. A PIECE SMALLER IN VOLUME THAN HALF AN EGG SHOULD BE USED. THE FOLLOWING BLESSING IS RECITED [WITH THE INTENTION THAT IT ALSO APPLIES TO THE MAROR WHICH WILL BE EATEN DURING THE MEAL] BEFORE THE VEGETABLE IS EATEN.

■ The vegetable used for Karpas is of lowly origin, from beneath the earth. Yet, it develops into an integral part of a sacred feast. So the lowly slave-nation grew to become the Chosen People. And so must each Jew, regardless of background, strive for ever greater spiritual heights.

BORUCH ato Adōnoy,

בָּרוּךְ אַתָּה יהוה

Blessed are You, HASHEM,

Elōhaynu melech ho-ōlom,

אֱלֹהֵינוּ מֶלֶךְ הָעוֹלָם,

our God, King of the universe,

bōray p'ri ho-adomo.

בּוֹרֵא פְּרִי הָאֲדָמָה.

Who creates the fruit of the ground.

יַחַץ / YACHATZ

BREAK THE MIDDLE MATZAH. THE HEAD OF THE HOUSEHOLD BREAKS THE MIDDLE MATZAH IN TWO. HE PUTS THE SMALLER PART BACK BETWEEN THE TWO WHOLE MATZOS, AND WRAPS UP THE LARGER PART FOR LATER USE AS THE AFIKOMAN. SOME BRIEFLY PLACE THE AFIKOMAN PORTION ON THEIR SHOULDERS, IN ACCORDANCE WITH THE BIBLICAL VERSE RECOUNTING THAT ISRAEL LEFT EGYPT CARRYING THEIR MATZOS ON THEIR SHOULDERS, AND SAY בְּבְהִלוּ יָצָאנוּ מִמִּצְרַיִם, "IN HASTE WE WENT OUT OF EGYPT."

■ The middle matzah is broken and half is set aside for later use. The symbolism of this is highlighted in the first paragraph of Maggid.

מַגִּיד / MAGGID

RECITE THE HAGGADAH. THE BROKEN MATZAH IS LIFTED FOR ALL TO SEE AS THE HEAD OF THE HOUSEHOLD BEGINS WITH THE FOLLOWING BRIEF EXPLANATION OF THE PROCEEDINGS.

■ The redemption is at this moment incomplete, we are free from Egypt, but we still look forward to have a future redemption when we will celebrate Passover, as of old, in the Holy Temple in a rebuilt Jerusalem.

HO lachmo anyo

הָא לַחְמָא עַנְיָא

This is the bread of affliction

di acholu avhosono

דִי אֲכָלוּ אַבְהָתָנָא

that our fathers ate

nirtzo   halayl   boraych   tzofun   shulchon ōraych   kōraych   morō

b'aro d'mitzro-yim.   בְּאַרְעָא דְמִצְרָיִם.

in the land of Egypt

Kol dichfin yaysay v'yaychōl,   כָּל דִּכְפִין יֵיתֵי וְיֵכוֹל,

Whoever is hungry — let him come and eat!

kol ditzrich yaysay v'yifsach.   כָּל דִּצְרִיךְ יֵיתֵי וְיִפְסַח.

Whoever is needy — let him come and celebrate Pesach!

Ho-shato hocho,   הָשַׁתָּא הָכָא,

Now, we are here;

l'shono habo-o   לְשָׁנָה הַבָּאָה

next year may we be

b'aro d'yisro-ayl.   בְּאַרְעָא דְיִשְׂרָאֵל.

in the Land of Israel!

Ho-shato avday,   הָשַׁתָּא עַבְדֵי,

Now, we are slaves;

l'shono habo-o b'nay chōrin.   לְשָׁנָה הַבָּאָה בְּנֵי חוֹרִין.

next year may we be free men!

THE SEDER PLATE IS REMOVED AND THE SECOND OF THE FOUR CUPS OF WINE IS POURED.
THE YOUNGEST PRESENT ASKS THE REASONS FOR THE EVENING'S UNUSUAL PROCEEDINGS.

■ The Story of the Exodus opens with a child's questions, for Scripture often
mentions this narrative in the form of a father's reply to his child's questions.

MAH NISHTANO   מַה נִּשְׁתַּנָּה

halailo ha-ze   הַלַּיְלָה הַזֶּה

Why is this night different

mikol halaylōs?   מִכָּל הַלֵּילוֹת?

from all other nights?

■ The Four Questions note the contradictory observances of the Seder.
We eat matzah and bitter herbs, which symbolize oppression and slavery,
but at the same time we dip our vegetables and recline on couches,
which indicate opulence and freedom!

1. Sheb'chol halaylōs   שֶׁבְּכָל הַלֵּילוֹת

On all other nights

onu ōch-lin chomaytz umatzo,   אָנוּ אוֹכְלִין חָמֵץ וּמַצָּה,

we may eat chametz and matzah,

atzo   mōtzi   roch'tzo   magio   yachatz   karpas   ur'chatz   kaɒaysh halailo ha-ze — kulō matzo.   הַלַּיְלָה הַזֶּה – כֻּלּוֹ מַצָּה.

but on this night — only matzah.

2. Sheb'chol halaylōs   **שֶׁבְּכָל** הַלֵּילוֹת

On all other nights

onu ōch-lin sh'or y'rokōs,   אָנוּ אוֹכְלִין שְׁאָר יְרָקוֹת,

we eat many vegetables,

halailo ha-ze — morōr.   הַלַּיְלָה הַזֶּה – מָרוֹר.

but on this night — we eat maror.

3. Sheb'chol halaylōs   **שֶׁבְּכָל** הַלֵּילוֹת

On all other nights

ayn onu matbilin   אֵין אָנוּ מַטְבִּילִין

we do not dip

afilu pa-am echos,   אֲפִילוּ פַּעַם אֶחָת,

even once,

halailo ha-ze — sh'tay f'omim.   הַלַּיְלָה הַזֶּה – שְׁתֵּי פְעָמִים.

but on this night — twice.

4. Sheb'chol halaylōs   **שֶׁבְּכָל** הַלֵּילוֹת

On all other nights

onu ōch-lin   אָנוּ אוֹכְלִין

we eat

bayn yōsh-vin uvayn m'subin,   בֵּין יוֹשְׁבִין וּבֵין מְסֻבִּין,

either sitting or reclining,

halailo ha-ze — kulonu m'subin.   הַלַּיְלָה הַזֶּה – כֻּלָּנוּ מְסֻבִּין.

but on this night — we all recline.

THE SEDER PLATE IS RETURNED. THE MATZOS ARE KEPT UNCOVERED AS THE HAGGADAH IS RECITED IN UNISON. THE HAGGADAH SHOULD BE TRANSLATED, IF NECESSARY, AND THE STORY OF THE EXODUS SHOULD BE AMPLIFIED UPON.

■ The child is first answered with a brief summary of the entire epoch —
"We were slaves, and then God freed us."
Subsequently, more and more details will be added to the narrative.

AVODIM hoyinu l'farōh   עֲבָדִים הָיִינוּ לְפַרְעֹה
     b'mitzro-yim.   בְּמִצְרַיִם,

We were slaves to Pharaoh in Egypt,

nirtzo   halayl   Boraych   tzofun   shulchon ōraych   kōraych   morō

vayōtzi-aynu Adōnoy Elōhaynu mishom

וַיּוֹצִיאֵנוּ יהוה אֱלֹהֵינוּ מִשָּׁם

but HASHEM our God took us out from there

b'yod chazoko uvizrō-a n'tuyo.

בְּיָד חֲזָקָה וּבִזְרֹעַ נְטוּיָה.

with a mighty hand and an outstretched arm.

V'ilu lō hōtzi Hakodōsh boruch hu

וְאִלּוּ לֹא הוֹצִיא הַקָּדוֹשׁ בָּרוּךְ הוּא

Had not the Holy One, Blessed is He, taken

es avōsaynu mimitzra-yim

אֶת אֲבוֹתֵינוּ מִמִּצְרַיִם,

our fathers out from Egypt,

haray onu uvonaynu

הֲרֵי אָנוּ וּבָנֵינוּ

then we, our children,

uv-nay vonaynu

וּבְנֵי בָנֵינוּ

and our children's children

m'shubodim hoyinu

מְשֻׁעְבָּדִים הָיִינוּ

would have remained enslaved

l'farōh b'mitzro-yim.

לְפַרְעֹה בְּמִצְרָיִם.

to Pharaoh in Egypt.

Va-afilu kulonu chachomim,

וַאֲפִילוּ כֻּלָּנוּ חֲכָמִים,

Even if we were all men of wisdom,

kulonu n'vōnim, kulonu z'kaynim,

כֻּלָּנוּ נְבוֹנִים, כֻּלָּנוּ זְקֵנִים,

understanding, experience,

kulonu yōd'im es hatōro,

כֻּלָּנוּ יוֹדְעִים אֶת הַתּוֹרָה,

and knowledge of the Torah,

mitzvo olaynu l'sapayr

מִצְוָה עָלֵינוּ לְסַפֵּר

it would still be an obligation upon us to tell

bitzi-as mitzra-yim.

בִּיצִיאַת מִצְרָיִם.

about the Exodus from Egypt.

V'chol hamarbe l'sapayr

וְכָל הַמַּרְבֶּה לְסַפֵּר

The more one tells

biytzi-as mitzra-yim

בִּיצִיאַת מִצְרַיִם,

about the Exodus from Egypt,

haray ze m'shuboch.

הֲרֵי זֶה מְשֻׁבָּח.

the more he is praiseworthy.

קַדֵּשׁ וּרְחַץ כַּרְפַּס יַחַץ מַגִּיד רָחְצָה מוֹצִיא מַ

tzo   mōtzi   roch'tzo   magid   yachatz   karpas   ur'chatz   kadaysh

■ Even great sages, who surely know the story, must recount it at great length. The most venerable sages of that time spend the entire night of Pesach recounting the story of the Exodus.

MA-ASE b'rabi eli-ezer   מַעֲשֶׂה בְּרַבִּי אֱלִיעֶזֶר

It happened that Rabbi Eliezer,

v'rabi y'hōshu-a   וְרַבִּי יְהוֹשֻׁעַ

Rabbi Yehoshua,

v'rabi elozor ben azaryo   וְרַבִּי אֶלְעָזָר בֶּן עֲזַרְיָה

Rabbi Elazar ben Azaryah,

v'rabi akivo v'rabi tarfōn   וְרַבִּי עֲקִיבָא וְרַבִּי טַרְפוֹן

Rabbi Akiva, and Rabbi Tarfon

sheho-yu m'subin bivnay v'rak,   שֶׁהָיוּ מְסֻבִּין בִּבְנֵי בְרַק,

were reclining (at the Seder) in Bnei Brak.

v'ho-yu m'sap'rim   וְהָיוּ מְסַפְּרִים

They discussed

bitzi-as mitzra-yim   בִּיצִיאַת מִצְרַיִם

the Exodus from Egypt

kol ōsō halailo.   כָּל אוֹתוֹ הַלַּיְלָה.

all that night

Ad shebo-u salmidayhem   עַד שֶׁבָּאוּ תַלְמִידֵיהֶם

until their students came

v'om'ru lohem: וְאָמְרוּ לָהֶם,

and said to them:

Rabōsaynu, higi-a z'man   רַבּוֹתֵינוּ הִגִּיעַ זְמַן

"Our teachers, the time [daybreak] has arrived

k'ri-as sh'ma shel shacharis.   קְרִיאַת שְׁמַע שֶׁל שַׁחֲרִית.

for the reading of the morning Shema."

■ One of the participants in the Bnei Brak Seder, Rabbi Elazar ben Azaryah, had a novel teaching about the requirement to remember the Exodus.

OMAR rabi elozor ben azaryo.   אָמַר רַבִּי אֶלְעָזָר בֶּן עֲזַרְיָה,

Rabbi Elazar, son of Azaryah, said:

Haray ani   הֲרֵי אֲנִי

I am like

nirtzo   halayl   BORaych   tzofun   shulchon ōraych   kōraych   morō

k'ven shivim shono,
a man of seventy,

v'lō zochisi
yet I was never able to convince my colleagues

shetay-omayr y'tzi-as mitzra-yim balaylōs,
that one is obliged to mention the Exodus at night

ad shed'roshoh ben zōmo,
until Ben Zoma explained it:

shene-emar,
It is stated [in the Torah]:

l'ma-an tizkōr
"That you may remember

es yōm tzays'cho
the day when you came out

may-eretz mitzra-yim
of the land of Egypt,

kōl y'may cha-yecho.
all the days of your life."

Y'may cha-yecho hayomim,
"The days of your life" merely refers to the days;

kōl y'may cha-yecho halaylōs.
"all the days of your life," on the other hand, includes the nights too.

Vachachomim ōm'rim
The Sages say:

y'may cha-yecho ho-ōlom ha-ze,
"The days of your life" indicates this life,

kōl y'may cha-yecho
but "all the days of your life"

l'hovi limōs hamoshi-ach.
includes the times of Mashiach too.

כְּבֶן שִׁבְעִים שָׁנָה,

וְלֹא זָכִיתִי

שֶׁתֵּאָמֵר יְצִיאַת מִצְרַיִם בַּלֵּילוֹת,

עַד שֶׁדְּרָשָׁהּ בֶּן זוֹמָא,

שֶׁנֶּאֱמַר,

לְמַעַן תִּזְכֹּר

אֶת יוֹם צֵאתְךָ

מֵאֶרֶץ מִצְרַיִם

כֹּל יְמֵי חַיֶּיךָ.

יְמֵי חַיֶּיךָ הַיָּמִים,

כֹּל יְמֵי חַיֶּיךָ הַלֵּילוֹת.

וַחֲכָמִים אוֹמְרִים,

יְמֵי חַיֶּיךָ הָעוֹלָם הַזֶּה,

כֹּל יְמֵי חַיֶּיךָ

לְהָבִיא לִימוֹת הַמָּשִׁיחַ.

■ From the various shades of expression in Scripture's description of the father-son dialogue, four types of offspring can be discerned.

BORUCH Hamokōm, boruch hu.   בָּרוּךְ הַמָּקוֹם, בָּרוּךְ הוּא.
Praised is the Ever-Present, praised is He!

atzo   mōtzi   Roch'tzo   magid   yachatz   karpas   ur'chatz   kadaysh

Boruch shenosan tōro   בָּרוּךְ שֶׁנָּתַן תּוֹרָה
Praised is He Who has given the Torah

l'amō yisro-ayl,   לְעַמּוֹ יִשְׂרָאֵל,
to His people Israel,

boruch hu.   בָּרוּךְ הוּא.
praised is He!

K'neged arbo-o vonim   כְּנֶגֶד אַרְבָּעָה בָנִים
  dib'ro sōro.   דִּבְּרָה תוֹרָה:
The Torah speaks of four sons:

Echod chochom,   אֶחָד חָכָם,
a wise one,

v'echod rosho,   וְאֶחָד רָשָׁע,
a wicked one,

v'echod tom,   וְאֶחָד תָּם,
a simple one,

v'echod she-aynō yōday-a lish-ōl.   וְאֶחָד שֶׁאֵינוֹ יוֹדֵעַ לִשְׁאוֹל.
and one who does not know how to ask.

■ The wise son seeks knowledge.

CHOCHOM mo hu ōmayr?   ?מָה הוּא אוֹמֵר **חָכָם**
What does the wise son say?

Mo ho-aydōs v'hachukim   מָה הָעֵדֹת וְהַחֻקִּים
  v'hamishpotim   וְהַמִּשְׁפָּטִים
"What are the testimonies, statutes and laws

asher tzivo Adōnoy   אֲשֶׁר צִוָּה יהוה
  Elōhaynu eschem?   אֱלֹהֵינוּ אֶתְכֶם?
that HASHEM our God has commanded you?"

V'af ato emor lō   וְאַף אַתָּה אֱמָר לוֹ
  k'hilchōs hapesach,   כְּהִלְכוֹת הַפֶּסַח,
Do then instruct him in the laws of Pesach,

ayn maftirin   אֵין מַפְטִירִין
that one may not eat anything

achar hapesach afikōmon.   אַחַר הַפֶּסַח אֲפִיקוֹמָן.
after eating the Pesach sacrifice!

NIRTZO   halayl   BORAYCH   tzofun   shulchon ōraych   kōraych   morō

■ The wicked son looks down on the beliefs of his people and scoffs.

ROSHO mo hu ōmayr?　　　　　　רָשָׁע מָה הוּא אוֹמֵר?
The wicked son — what does he say?

Mo ho-avōdo hazōs lochem?　　　　מָה הָעֲבֹדָה הַזֹּאת לָכֶם?
"What does this service mean to you?"

Lochem v'lō lō.　　　　　　　　　　לָכֶם וְלֹא לוֹ,
"To you" (he says) — but not to him!

Ul-fi shehōtzi es atzmō　　　　וּלְפִי שֶׁהוֹצִיא אֶת עַצְמוֹ
Therefore, because he has excluded himself

min hak'lol　　　　　　　　　　　　מִן הַכְּלָל,
from the community,

kofar b'ikor.　　　　　　　　　　כָּפַר בְּעִקָּר —
he has denied the foundation of our faith;

V'af ato hakhay es shinov　　　וְאַף אַתָּה הַקְהֵה אֶת שִׁנָּיו
consequently you must blunt his teeth

ve-emor lō,　　　　　　　　　　　　וֶאֱמָר לוֹ,
and reply to him:

ba-avur ze oso Adōnoy li　　　בַּעֲבוּר זֶה עָשָׂה יהוה לִי
"It is because of this that HASHEM did for me

b'tzaysi mimitzro-yim.　　　　בְּצֵאתִי מִמִּצְרָיִם.
when I went out from Egypt";

Li v'lō lō.　　　　　　　　　　　　לִי וְלֹא לוֹ,
"for me" (you say), but not for him —

Ilu ho-yo shom lō ho-yo nigol.　אִלּוּ הָיָה שָׁם לֹא הָיָה נִגְאָל.
had he been there, he would not have been redeemed.

■ The simple son asks a simple question.

TOM mo hu ōmayr?　　　　　　תָּם מָה הוּא אוֹמֵר?
The simple son — what does he say?

Ma zōs?　　　　　　　　　　　　　　מַה זֹּאת?
"What does this mean?"

V'omarto aylov　　　　　　　　　　וְאָמַרְתָּ אֵלָיו,
To him you shall say:

atzo　mōtzi　roch'tzo　magro　yachatz　karpas　ur'chatz　kadaysh
קַדֵּשׁ וּרְחַץ כַּרְפַּס יַחַץ מַגִּיד רָחְצָה מוֹצִיא מַצָּ

b'chōzek yod hōtzi-onu Adōnoy

בְּחֹזֶק יָד הוֹצִיאָנוּ יהוה

"With a strong hand did HASHEM bring us out

mimitzra-yim mibays avodim.

מִמִּצְרַיִם מִבֵּית עֲבָדִים.

from Egypt, from the house of bondage."

■ If the child does not ask, the parent must teach.

V'SHE-AYNŌ yōday-a lishōl

וְשֶׁאֵינוֹ יוֹדֵעַ לִשְׁאוֹל,

As for the son who does not know what to ask,

at p'sach lō,

אַתְּ פְּתַח לוֹ,

you must begin to speak to him,

shene-emar:

שֶׁנֶּאֱמַר,

as it is stated:

v'higadto l'vincho ba-yōm hahu

וְהִגַּדְתָּ לְבִנְךָ בַּיּוֹם הַהוּא

"You shall tell your son on that day

laymōr

לֵאמֹר,

saying:

ba-avur ze oso Adōnoy li

בַּעֲבוּר זֶה עָשָׂה יהוה לִי

'Because of this, HASHEM did so for me

b'tzaysi mimitzro-yim.

בְּצֵאתִי מִמִּצְרָיִם.

when I went out from Egypt.'"

■ God instructed Moses on the first of Nissan to prepare the nation
for its imminent departure from Egypt.

YOCHŌL mayrōsh chōdesh,

יָכוֹל מֵרֹאשׁ חֹדֶשׁ,

*One might think that the obligation to talk about the Exodus from Egypt
applies from the first day of the month of Nissan;*

talmud lōmar ba-yōm hahu.

תַּלְמוּד לוֹמַר בַּיּוֹם הַהוּא.

therefore the Torah says: "on that day."

I ba-yōm hahu

אִי בַּיּוֹם הַהוּא,

The expression "that day"

yochōl mib'ōd yōm,

יָכוֹל מִבְּעוֹד יוֹם,

might be understood to refer to daytime;

talmud lōmar ba-avur ze.

תַּלְמוּד לוֹמַר בַּעֲבוּר זֶה.

therefore, the Torah adds that the father should say: "because of this";

נִרְצָה   חַלֵּל   בּוֹרֵךְ   צָפוּן   בֵּרֵךְ   הַלֵּל   מַצָּה

nirtzo   halayl   bōraych   tzofun   shulchon ōraych   kōraych   morō

Ba-avur ze lō omarti   בַּעֲבוּר זֶה לֹא אָמַרְתִּי

that expression can be used

elo b'sho-o   אֶלָּא בְּשָׁעָה

only at a time

she-yaysh matzo umorōr   שֶׁיֵּשׁ מַצָּה וּמָרוֹר

munochim l'fonecho.   מֻנָּחִים לְפָנֶיךָ.

when matzah and maror actually lie before you.

■ The spiritual greatness of our lofty Abrahamitic heritage is contrasted with the moral decay of our earliest ancestors.

MIT'CHILO   מִתְּחִלָּה,

In the beginning

ōv'day avōdo zoro   עוֹבְדֵי עֲבוֹדָה זָרָה

ho-yu avōsaynu,   הָיוּ אֲבוֹתֵינוּ,

our fathers were worshipers of idols,

v'achshov   וְעַכְשָׁו

but now

kayr'vonu Hamokōm la-avōdosō,   קֵרְבָנוּ הַמָּקוֹם לַעֲבוֹדָתוֹ.

the Ever-Present has brought us to His service,

shene-emar: שֶׁנֶּאֱמַר,

as [the verse] states:

vayōmer y'hōshu-a   וַיֹּאמֶר יְהוֹשֻׁעַ

"And Joshua spoke

el kol ho-om   אֶל כָּל הָעָם,

to the whole people:

kō omar Adōnoy Elōhay yisro-ayl,   כֹּה אָמַר יהוה אֱלֹהֵי יִשְׂרָאֵל,

Thus has HASHEM, God of Israel, spoken:

b'ayver hanohor   בְּעֵבֶר הַנָּהָר

'Beyond the River (Euphrates),

yosh'vu avōsaychem may-ōlom,   יָשְׁבוּ אֲבוֹתֵיכֶם מֵעוֹלָם,

Your fathers dwelt in olden times

terach avi avrohom   תֶּרַח אֲבִי אַבְרָהָם

va-avi nochōr   וַאֲבִי נָחוֹר,

Terach, the father of Abraham and the father of Nachor,

קָדֵשׁ וּרְחַץ כַּרְפַּס יַחַץ מַגִּיד רָחְצָה מוֹצִיא מַצָּ

atzo   mōtzi   rōch'tzo   **magid**   yachatz   karpas   ur'chatz   kadaysh vaya-avdu elōhim achayrim.

וַיַּעַבְדוּ אֱלֹהִים אֲחֵרִים.

and they served other gods.

Vo-ekach es avichem es
avrohom may-ayver hanohor

וָאֶקַּח אֶת אֲבִיכֶם אֶת
אַבְרָהָם מֵעֵבֶר הַנָּהָר,

And I took your father Abraham from beyond the River

vo-ōlaych ōsō
b'chol eretz k'no-an

וָאוֹלֵךְ אוֹתוֹ
בְּכָל אֶרֶץ כְּנָעַן,

and led him throughout all the land of Canaan,

vo-arbe es zarō

וָאַרְבֶּה אֶת זַרְעוֹ,

and I multiplied his seed

vo-eten lō es yitzchok.

וָאֶתֵּן לוֹ אֶת יִצְחָק.

and gave him Isaac.

Vo-etayn l'yitzchok es ya-akōv
v'es aysov

וָאֶתֵּן לְיִצְחָק אֶת יַעֲקֹב
וְאֶת עֵשָׂו,

And I gave to Isaac — Jacob and Esau;

vo-etayn l'aysov es har say-ir
loreshes ōsō

וָאֶתֵּן לְעֵשָׂו אֶת הַר שֵׂעִיר
לָרֶשֶׁת אוֹתוֹ,

and I gave to Esau Mount Seir, to possess it,

v'ya-akōv uvonov yor'du mitzro-yim. וְיַעֲקֹב וּבָנָיו יָרְדוּ מִצְרָיְמָה.

and Jacob and his sons went down to Egypt.' "

■ Despite Israel's descent to Egypt, God's promise to Abraham was not forgotten.

BORUCH shōmayr havtochosō   בָּרוּךְ שׁוֹמֵר הַבְטָחָתוֹ

Blessed is He Who keeps His assurance

l'yisro-ayl,

לְיִשְׂרָאֵל,

to Israel,

boruch hu.

בָּרוּךְ הוּא.

blessed is He!

Shehakodōsh boruch hu

שֶׁהַקָּדוֹשׁ בָּרוּךְ הוּא

For the Holy One, Blessed is He,

chishav es hakaytz

חִשַּׁב אֶת הַקֵּץ,

planned the end of their bondage,

la-asōs

לַעֲשׂוֹת

in order to do

נרצו   halayl   BORaych   tzofun   shulchon ōraych   kōraych   morо
nirtzo

k'mo she-omar l'avrohom ovinu   כְּמָה שֶׁאָמַר לְאַבְרָהָם אָבִינוּ
as He had said to our father Abraham

biv-ris bayn hab'sorim,   בִּבְרִית בֵּין הַבְּתָרִים,
at the Covenant between the Portions,

shene-emar: שֶׁנֶּאֱמַר,
as it says:

va-yōmer l'avrom   וַיֹּאמֶר לְאַבְרָם,
"And He said to Abram:

yodō-a tayda   יָדְעַ תֵּדַע
'You should know for certain

ki gayr yih-ye zar-acho   כִּי גֵר יִהְיֶה זַרְעֲךָ
that your descendants shall be strangers

b'eretz lō lohem   בְּאֶרֶץ לֹא לָהֶם,
in a land that is not theirs,

va-avodum v'inu ōsom   וַעֲבָדוּם וְעִנּוּ אֹתָם,
and they shall serve them, and they shall treat them harshly,

arba may-ōs shono.   אַרְבַּע מֵאוֹת שָׁנָה.
for four hundred years;

V'gam es hagōy asher ya-avōdu   וְגַם אֶת הַגּוֹי אֲשֶׁר יַעֲבֹדוּ
don onōchi   דָּן אָנֹכִי,
but I will also judge the nation that they shall serve,

v'acharay chayn   וְאַחֲרֵי כֵן
and afterwards

yaytz'u bir-chush godōl.   יֵצְאוּ בִּרְכֻשׁ גָּדוֹל.
they shall come out with great wealth.'"

THE MATZOS ARE COVERED AND THE CUPS LIFTED AS THE FOLLOWING PARAGRAPH IS
PROCLAIMED JOYOUSLY. ON ITS CONCLUSION, THE CUPS ARE PUT DOWN AND
THE MATZOS ARE UNCOVERED.

■ Indeed, that promise has stood by us in all generations,
through countless persecutions.

V'HI SHE-OM'DO   וְהִיא שֶׁעָמְדָה
And it is this that has stood by

la-avōsaynu v'lonu.   לַאֲבוֹתֵינוּ וְלָנוּ,
our fathers and us;

Shelō echod bilvod   שֶׁלֹּא אֶחָד בִּלְבָד
for not only one

קַדֵּשׁ וּרְחַץ כַּרְפַּס יַחַץ מַגִּיד רָחְצָה מוֹצִיא מַצָּה
atzo   mōtzi   roch'tzo   magid   yachatz   karpas   ur'chatz   kadaysh

omad olaynu l'chalōsaynu　　　　　עָמַד עָלֵינוּ לְכַלּוֹתֵנוּ.

has risen up against us to destroy us,

elo sheb'chol dōr vodōr　　　　　אֶלָּא שֶׁבְּכָל דּוֹר וָדוֹר

but in all ages

ōm'dim olaynu l'chalōsaynu　　　　עוֹמְדִים עָלֵינוּ לְכַלּוֹתֵנוּ,

they rise up against us to destroy us;

v'Hakodōsh boruch hu　　　　　וְהַקָּדוֹשׁ בָּרוּךְ הוּא

and the Holy One, Blessed is He,

matzilaynu miyodom.　　　　　מַצִּילֵנוּ מִיָּדָם.

rescues us from their hands.

■ Even before the Exodus, that promise protected us from Laban, whose evil was, in a sense, more potent that Pharaoh's.

TZAY ul-mad　　　　　צֵא וּלְמַד

Go and learn

ma bikaysh lovon ho-arami　　　מַה בִּקֵּשׁ לָבָן הָאֲרַמִּי

what Laban the Aramean planned

la-asōs l'ya-akōv ovinu.　　　　לַעֲשׂוֹת לְיַעֲקֹב אָבִינוּ,

to do to our father Jacob;

Sheparō lō gozar　　　　　שֶׁפַּרְעֹה לֹא גָזַר

for Pharaoh decreed

elo al haz'chorim　　　　　אֶלָּא עַל הַזְּכָרִים,

only that the male (children) should be put to death,

v'lovon bikaysh la-akōr es hakōl.　וְלָבָן בִּקֵּשׁ לַעֲקוֹר אֶת הַכֹּל.

but Laban had planned to uproot all,

Shene-emar　　　　　שֶׁנֶּאֱמַר...

as it says:

■ Details of Israel's descent, oppression, prayers, and deliverance are now added in a word-by-word exposition of four verses in *Deuteronomy*. The first verse speaks of the descent to Egypt.

ARAMI ōvayd ovi　　　　　אֲרַמִּי אֹבֵד אָבִי,

"The Aramean sought to destroy my father,

va-yayred mitzrai-mo　　　　　וַיֵּרֶד מִצְרַיְמָה

and the latter went down to Egypt

נחור　כֹּרֵךְ　שֻׁלְחָן עוֹרֵךְ　צָפוּן　בָּרֵךְ　הַלֵּל　נִרְצָה

nirtzo　halayl　boraych　tzofun　shulchon ōraych　kōraych　moro

va-yogor shom bimsay m'ot,

וַיָּגָר שָׁם בִּמְתֵי מְעָט,

and sojourned there, with a family few in number;

va-y'hi shom l'gōy

וַיְהִי שָׁם לְגוֹי,

and he became there a nation,

godōl otzum vorov.

גָּדוֹל עָצוּם וָרָב.

great, mighty and numerous."

VA-YAYRED MITZRAI-MO — וַיֵּרֶד מִצְרַיְמָה

"And he went down to Egypt" —

onus al pi hadibur.

אָנוּס עַל פִּי הַדִּבּוּר.

compelled by Divine decree.

■ Our ancestors' descent to Egypt was part of the Divine plan. They thought their stay would be short.

VAYOGOR SHOM. — וַיָּגָר שָׁם

"And he sojourned there" —

M'lamayd

מְלַמֵּד

which teaches

shelō yorad ya-akōv ovinu

שֶׁלֹּא יָרַד יַעֲקֹב אָבִינוּ

that our father Jacob did not go down

l'hishtakay-a b'mitzra-yim,

לְהִשְׁתַּקֵּעַ בְּמִצְרַיִם,

to Egypt to settle there permanently,

elo logur shom,

אֶלָּא לָגוּר שָׁם.

but merely to stay there for a time,

shene-emar:

שֶׁנֶּאֱמַר,

as it says:

vayōm'ru el parō

וַיֹּאמְרוּ אֶל פַּרְעֹה,

"And they (the sons of Jacob) said to Pharaoh:

logur bo-oretz bonu

לָגוּר בָּאָרֶץ בָּאנוּ,

'We have come to sojourn in this land

ki ayn mire

כִּי אֵין מִרְעֶה

for there is no pasture

latzōn asher la-avodecho,

לַצֹּאן אֲשֶׁר לַעֲבָדֶיךָ,

for the flocks that belong to your servants,

קַדֵּשׁ וּרְחַץ כַּרְפַּס יַחַץ מַגִּיד רָחְצָה מוֹצִיא מַצָ
atzo   mōtzi   Roch'tzo   MAGID   yachatz   karpas   ur'chatz   kadaysh

ki chovayd horo-ov b'eretz k'no-an, כִּי כָבֵד הָרָעָב בְּאֶרֶץ כְּנָעַן,
for the famine is severe in the land of Canaan;

v'ato yaysh'vu no avodecho וְעַתָּה יֵשְׁבוּ נָא עֲבָדֶיךָ
and now please let your servants dwell

b'eretz gōshen. בְּאֶרֶץ גֹּשֶׁן.
in the land of Goshen.'"

■ They were few in number . . .

BIMSAY M'OT. — בְּמְתֵי מְעָט

"With few in number" —

K'mo shene-emar: כְּמָה שֶׁנֶּאֱמַר,
as it says:

b'shiv-im nefesh בְּשִׁבְעִים נֶפֶשׁ
With seventy persons;

yor'du avōsecho mitzroi-mo יָרְדוּ אֲבֹתֶיךָ מִצְרַיְמָה,
"your fathers went down to Egypt

v'ato som'cho Adōnoy Elohecho וְעַתָּה שָׂמְךָ יהוה אֱלֹהֶיךָ
and now HASHEM, your God, has made you

k'chōch'vay hashoma-yim lorōv. כְּכוֹכְבֵי הַשָּׁמַיִם לָרֹב.
as numerous as the stars of heaven."

■ but remained distinctive . . .

VA-Y'HI SHOM L'GŌY. — וַיְהִי שָׁם לְגוֹי

"And he became there a nation" —

M'lamayd מְלַמֵּד
which teaches

sheho-yu yisro-ayl שֶׁהָיוּ יִשְׂרָאֵל
that the Jews

m'tzu-yonim shom. מְצֻיָּנִים שָׁם.
were distinctive there.

■ powerful . . .

GODŌL, OTZUM. — גָּדוֹל עָצוּם

"Great, mighty" —

K'mo shene-emar:
as it says:

כְּמָה שֶׁנֶּאֱמַר,

uv'nay yisro-ayl poru

וּבְנֵי יִשְׂרָאֵל פָּרוּ

"And the children of Israel were fruitful

vayish-r'tzu va-yirbu

וַיִּשְׁרְצוּ וַיִּרְבּוּ

and increased abundantly and multiplied

vaya-atzmu bim-ōd m'ōd

וַיַּעַצְמוּ בִּמְאֹד מְאֹד,

and became very, very mighty;

vatimolay ho-oretz ōsom.

וַתִּמָּלֵא הָאָרֶץ אֹתָם.

and the land was filled with them."

■ and numerous.

VOROV. — וָרָב

"And numerous" —

K'mo shene-emar:
as it says:

כְּמָה שֶׁנֶּאֱמַר,

r'vovo k'tzemach hasode

רְבָבָה כְּצֶמַח הַשָּׂדֶה

"Like the plants of the field

n'satich

נְתַתִּיךְ,

I made you thrive,

vatirbi vatigd'li

וַתִּרְבִּי וַתִּגְדְּלִי

and you grew big and tall,

vatovō-i ba-adi ado-yim

וַתָּבֹאִי בַּעֲדִי עֲדָיִים,

and you came to be of great charm,

shoda-yim nochōnu

שָׁדַיִם נָכֹנוּ

beautiful of form,

us-oraych tzimay-ach

וּשְׂעָרֵךְ צִמֵּחַ,

and your hair was grown long;

v'at ayrōm v'eryo.

וְאַתְּ עֵרֹם וְעֶרְיָה;

but you were naked and bare.

Vo-e-evōr ola-yich vo-er-aych

וָאֶעֱבֹר עָלַיִךְ וָאֶרְאֵךְ

And I passed over you and I saw you

misbōseses b'domo-yich,

מִתְבּוֹסֶסֶת בְּדָמָיִךְ,

downtrodden in your blood

vo-ōmar loch b'doma-yich cha-yi,   וָאֹמַר לָךְ, בְּדָמַיִךְ חֲיִי,
and I said to you: 'through your blood you shall live';

vo-ōmar loch b'doma-yich cha-yi.   וָאֹמַר לָךְ, בְּדָמַיִךְ חֲיִי.
and I said to you: 'through your blood you shall live.' "

■ The second verse describes the oppressiveness of the Egyptians.

VA-YORAY-U ōsonu hamitzrim   **וַיָּרֵעוּ אֹתָנוּ הַמִּצְרִים,**
"The Egyptians ill-treated us,

vai-anunu   **וַיְעַנּוּנוּ,**
oppressed us

va-yit'nu olaynu avōdo kosho.   **וַיִּתְּנוּ עָלֵינוּ עֲבֹדָה קָשָׁה.**
and laid heavy labors upon us."

■ Subtly, with guile, the Egyptians laid their plans.

VA-YORAY-U ōsonu hamitzrim.   — **וַיָּרֵעוּ אֹתָנוּ הַמִּצְרִים**
"The Egyptians ill-treated us" —

K'mo shene-emar: כְּמָה שֶׁנֶּאֱמַר,
as it says:

hovo nischak'mo lō   הָבָה נִתְחַכְּמָה לוֹ,
"Come, let us deal cunningly with them,

pen yirbe   פֶּן יִרְבֶּה,
lest they multiply,

v'ho-yo ki sikreno milchomo   וְהָיָה כִּי תִקְרֶאנָה מִלְחָמָה,
and, if we should happen to be at war,

v'nōsaf gam hu al sōn'aynu   וְנוֹסַף גַּם הוּא עַל שֹׂנְאֵינוּ,
and they will join our enemies,

v'nilcham bonu   וְנִלְחַם בָּנוּ,
and fight against us

v'olo min ho-oretz.   וְעָלָה מִן הָאָרֶץ.
and go out of the country."

■ They forced back-breaking labor upon us.

VAI-ANUNU.   — **וַיְעַנּוּנוּ**
"They oppressed us" —

nirtzo   halayl   Boraych   tzofun   shulchon ōraych   kōraych   morō

K'mo shene-emar:
כְּמָה שֶׁנֶּאֱמַר,
as it says:

va-yosimu olov soray misim
וַיָּשִׂימוּ עָלָיו שָׂרֵי מִסִּים,
"They placed taskmasters over them,

l'ma-an anōsō b'sivlōsom
לְמַעַן עַנֹּתוֹ בְּסִבְלֹתָם,
to oppress them with their impositions,

va-yiven oray misk'nōs l'farō
וַיִּבֶן עָרֵי מִסְכְּנוֹת לְפַרְעֹה,
and they built store-cities for Pharaoh,

es pisōm v'es ra-amsays.
אֶת פִּתֹם וְאֶת רַעַמְסֵס.
Pisom and Ramses."

VA-YIT'NU olaynu avōdo kosho. — וַיִּתְּנוּ עָלֵינוּ עֲבֹדָה קָשָׁה
"They laid heavy labors upon us" —

K'mo shene-emar:
כְּמָה שֶׁנֶּאֱמַר,
as it says:

va-ya-avidu mitzra-yim
וַיַּעֲבִדוּ מִצְרַיִם
"The Egyptians enslaved

es b'nay yisro-ayl
אֶת בְּנֵי יִשְׂרָאֵל
the Children of Israel

b'forech.
בְּפָרֶךְ.
with crushing harshness."

■ The third verse speaks of our prayers and God's response.

VANITZAK el Adōnoy
וַנִּצְעַק אֶל יהוה
"We cried to HASHEM,

Elōhay avōsaynu
אֱלֹהֵי אֲבֹתֵינוּ,
the God of our fathers,

va-yishma Adōnoy es kōlaynu
וַיִּשְׁמַע יהוה אֶת קֹלֵנוּ,
and HASHEM heard our voice.

va-yar es on-yaynu
וַיַּרְא אֶת עָנְיֵנוּ,
He saw our ill-treatment,

v'es amolaynu
וְאֶת עֲמָלֵנוּ,
our burden

v'es lachatzaynu.
וְאֶת לַחֲצֵנוּ.
and our oppression."

קַדֵּשׁ וּרְחַץ כַּרְפַּס יַחַץ מַגִּיד רָחְצָה מוֹצִיא מַצָּה
atzo mōtzi roch'tzo magid yachatz karpas ur'chatz kadaysh

■ When the slave labor imposed upon us became unbearable, we cried to God.

VANITZAK el Adōnoy — וַנִּצְעַק אֶל יהוה

"We cried to HASHEM,

Elōhay avōsaynu. — אֱלֹהֵי אֲבֹתֵינוּ

the God of our fathers —

K'mo shene-emar: — כְּמָה שֶׁנֶּאֱמַר,

as it says:

vai-hi va-yomim horabim hohaym — וַיְהִי בַיָּמִים הָרַבִּים הָהֵם,

"It came to pass during that long period

va-yomos melech mitzra-yim — וַיָּמָת מֶלֶךְ מִצְרַיִם,

that the king of Egypt died,

va-yay-on'chu v'nay yisro-ayl — וַיֵּאָנְחוּ בְנֵי יִשְׂרָאֵל

and the children of Israel groaned

min ho-avōdo — מִן הָעֲבֹדָה,

because of the bondage,

va-yiz-oku — וַיִּזְעָקוּ,

and they cried,

vata-al shavosom el ho-Elōhim — וַתַּעַל שַׁוְעָתָם אֶל הָאֱלֹהִים

and their prayers rose up to God

min ho-avōdo. — מִן הָעֲבֹדָה.

because of the servitude."

■ He listened and recalled His covenant with our forebears.

VA-YISHMA Adōnoy es kōlaynu. — וַיִּשְׁמַע יהוה אֶת קֹלֵנוּ

"HASHEM heard our voice" —

K'mo shene-emar: — כְּמָה שֶׁנֶּאֱמַר,

as it says:

va-yishma Elōhim es na-akosom — וַיִּשְׁמַע אֱלֹהִים אֶת נַאֲקָתָם,

"God heard their moaning

va-yizkōr Elōhim es b'riso — וַיִּזְכֹּר אֱלֹהִים אֶת בְּרִיתוֹ

and God recalled His covenant

es avrohom — אֶת אַבְרָהָם,

with Abraham,

es yitzchok

אֶת יִצְחָק,

Isaac

v'es ya-akōv.

וְאֶת יַעֲקֹב.

and Jacob."

■ He saw how our families were disrupted . . .

VA-YAR es on-yaynu.

וַיַּרְא אֶת עָנְיֵנוּ –

"He saw our ill-treatment" —

Zō p'rishus derech eretz.

זוֹ פְּרִישׁוּת דֶּרֶךְ אֶרֶץ,

this refers to the breaking up of their family life,

K'mo shene-emar:

כְּמָה שֶׁנֶּאֱמַר,

as it says:

va-yar Elōhim es b'nay yisro-ayl,

וַיַּרְא אֱלֹהִים אֶת בְּנֵי יִשְׂרָאֵל,

"God looked upon the children of Israel

va-yayda Elōhim.

וַיֵּדַע אֱלֹהִים.

and God took note."

■ how our children were killed . . .

V'ES AMOLAYNU.

וְאֶת עֲמָלֵנוּ –

"Our burden" —

Aylu habonim.

אֵלוּ הַבָּנִים,

this refers to the children,

K'mo shene-emar:

כְּמָה שֶׁנֶּאֱמַר,

as it says:

kol habayn ha-yilōd

כָּל הַבֵּן הַיִּלּוֹד

"Every newborn son

hai-ōro tashlichuhu

הַיְאֹרָה תַּשְׁלִיכֻהוּ,

shall you cast into the river

v'chol habas t'cha-yun.

וְכָל הַבַּת תְּחַיּוּן.

and every daughter you shall let live."

■ and how we suffered oppression.

V'ES LACHATZAYNU.

וְאֶת לַחֲצֵנוּ –

"Our oppression" —

atzo   mōtzi   roch'tzo   magio   yachatz   karpas   ur'chatz   kadaysh   קַדֵּשׁ וּרְחַץ כַּרְפַּס יַחַץ מַגִּיד רָחְצָה מוֹצִיא מַ

Zō had'chak.

זוֹ הַדְּדֻחַק,

this refers to the pressure

K'mo shene-emar:

כְּמָה שֶׁנֶּאֱמַר,

as it says:

v'gam ro-isi es halachatz

וְגַם רָאִיתִי אֶת הַלַּחַץ

"I have also seen the oppression

asher mitzra-yim lōchatzim ōsom.

אֲשֶׁר מִצְרַיִם לֹחֲצִים אֹתָם.

with which the Egyptians oppress them."

■ The fourth verse tells of the deliverance.

VA-YŌTZI-AYNU Adōnoy

וַיּוֹצִאֵנוּ יהוה

mimitzra-yim

מִמִּצְרַיִם

"HASHEM brought us out of Egypt

b'yod chazoko

בְּיָד חֲזָקָה,

with a mighty hand,

uvizrō-a n'tuyo

וּבִזְרֹעַ נְטוּיָה,

with an outstretched arm,

uv-mōro godōl

וּבְמֹרָא גָּדֹל,

with great fearfulness,

uv-ōsōs uv'mōf'sim.

וּבְאֹתוֹת וּבְמֹפְתִים.

with signs and with wonders."

■ No angel, no agent — only God, Himself, effected the redemption.

VAYŌTZI-AYNU Adōnoy

וַיּוֹצִאֵנוּ יהוה

mi-mitzra-yim.

מִמִּצְרַיִם —

"HASHEM brought us out of Egypt" —

Lō al y'day maloch

לֹא עַל יְדֵי מַלְאָךְ,

not through an angel,

v'lō al y'day sorof

וְלֹא עַל יְדֵי שָׂרָף,

not through a seraph

v'lō al y'day sholi-ach.

וְלֹא עַל יְדֵי שָׁלִיחַ,

and not through a messenger,

Elo Hakodōsh Boruch Hu

אֶלָּא הַקָּדוֹשׁ בָּרוּךְ הוּא

but the Holy One, Blessed is He,

bichvōdō uv'atzmō.

בִּכְבוֹדוֹ וּבְעַצְמוֹ.

He alone, in His glory,

Shene-emar:

שֶׁנֶּאֱמַר,

as it says:

v'ovarti v'eretz mitzra-yim
  balai-lo ha-ze

וְעָבַרְתִּי בְאֶרֶץ מִצְרַיִם
בַּלַּיְלָה הַזֶּה,

"I will pass through the land of Egypt in that night,

v'hikaysi chol b'chōr
  b'eretz mitzra-yim

וְהִכֵּיתִי כָל בְּכוֹר
בְּאֶרֶץ מִצְרַיִם

and I will slay every firstborn in the land of Egypt,

may-odom v'ad b'haymo

מֵאָדָם וְעַד בְּהֵמָה,

from man to beast,

uv'chol elōhay mitzra-yim

וּבְכָל אֱלֹהֵי מִצְרַיִם

and against all the gods of Egypt,

e-ese sh'fotim.

אֶעֱשֶׂה שְׁפָטִים,

I will execute judgment

Ani Adōnoy.

אֲנִי יהוה.

I, HASHEM.

V'ovarti v'eretz mitzra-yim
  balai-lo ha-ze.

וְעָבַרְתִּי בְאֶרֶץ מִצְרַיִם
בַּלַּיְלָה הַזֶּה —

"I will pass through the land of Egypt," on that night —

Ani v'lō maloch.

אֲנִי וְלֹא מַלְאָךְ.

I, and no angel;

V'hikaysi chol b'chōr
  b'eretz mitzra-yim.

וְהִכֵּיתִי כָל בְּכוֹר
בְּאֶרֶץ מִצְרַיִם —

"I will slay every firstborn in the land of Egypt,"

Ani v'lō sorof.

אֲנִי וְלֹא שָׂרָף.

I, and no seraph;

Uv'chol elōhay mitzra-yim

וּבְכָל אֱלֹהֵי מִצְרַיִם

"and against all the gods of Egypt,

e-ese sh'fotim.

אֶעֱשֶׂה שְׁפָטִים —

I will execute judgment"

Ani v'lō hasholi-ach.

אֲנִי וְלֹא הַשָּׁלִיחַ.

I, and no messenger;

קַדֵּשׁ וּרְחַץ כַּרְפַּס יַחַץ מַגִּיד רָחְצָה מוֹצִיא מַ
tzo   mōtzi   rōch'tzo   maGID   yachatz   karpas   ur'chatz   kaDaysh

Ani Adōnoy.

"I, Hashem,

Ani hu v'lō achayr.

it is I and no other."

אֲנִי יהוה —

אֲנִי הוּא, וְלֹא אַחֵר.

■ His hand smote the animals that the Egyptians had worshiped as gods.

B'YOD chazoko.

"With a mighty hand" —

Zō hadever.

this refers to the pestilence,

K'mo shene-emar:

as it says:

hinay yad Adōnoy

"Behold, the hand of Hashem

hōyo b'mikn'cho asher basode

will be upon your cattle in the field,

basusim bachamōrim bag'malim

upon the horses, asses and camels,

babokor uvatzōn

the oxen and the sheep,

dever kovayd m'ōd.

a very severe pestilence."

בְּיָד חֲזָקָה —

זוֹ הַדֶּבֶר,

כְּמָה שֶׁנֶּאֱמַר,

הִנֵּה יַד יהוה

הוֹיָה בְּמִקְנְךָ אֲשֶׁר בַּשָּׂדֶה,

בַּסּוּסִים בַּחֲמֹרִים בַּגְּמַלִּים

בַּבָּקָר וּבַצֹּאן,

דֶּבֶר כָּבֵד מְאֹד.

■ His sword slew their firstborn.

UVIZRŌ-A n'tuyo.

"With an outstretched arm" —

Zō hacherev.

that is the sword,

K'mo shene-emar:

as it says:

v'charbō sh'lufo b'yodō

"His drawn sword in His hand,

n'tuyo al y'rusholo-yim.

outstretched over Jerusalem."

וּבִזְרֹעַ נְטוּיָה —

זוֹ הַחֶרֶב,

כְּמָה שֶׁנֶּאֱמַר,

וְחַרְבּוֹ שְׁלוּפָה בְּיָדוֹ,

נְטוּיָה עַל יְרוּשָׁלָיִם.

nirtzo   halayl   Boraych   tzofun   shulchon ōraych   kōraych   morō

■ He revealed Himself by extricating the Israelites from among the Egyptians,

UV-MŌRO godōl.
"With great fearfulness" —

Zō giluy sh'chino.
this refers to the revelation of the Divine Presence,

K'mo shene-emar:
as it says:

ō haniso Elōhim
"Or has God ever sought

lovō lokachas lō
to come and take unto Himself

gōy mikerev gōy
one nation from the midst of another nation,

b'masōs b'ōsōs uv-mōf'sim
with trials, signs and wonders,

uv-milchomo uv-yod chazoko
with war and a mighty hand,

uvizrō-a n'tuyo
and an outstretched arm

uv-mōro-im g'dōlim
and awesome manifestations,

k'chōl asher oso lochem
as He did for you

Adōnoy Elōhaychem
— HASHEM, your God —

b'mitzra-yim l'aynecho.
in Egypt before your eyes.

■ and in the plagues invoked by Moses' staff . . .

UV-ŌSŌS.
"With signs" —

Ze hama-te.
this refers to the staff,

K'mo shene-emar:
as it is says:

וּבְמֹרָא גָּדֹל —

זוֹ גִּלּוּי שְׁכִינָה,

כְּמָה שֶׁנֶּאֱמַר,

אוֹ הֲנִסָּה אֱלֹהִים

לָבוֹא לָקַחַת לוֹ

גּוֹי מִקֶּרֶב גּוֹי,

בְּמַסֹּת, בְּאֹתֹת, וּבְמוֹפְתִים,

וּבְמִלְחָמָה, וּבְיָד חֲזָקָה,

וּבִזְרוֹעַ נְטוּיָה,

וּבְמוֹרָאִים גְּדֹלִים,

כְּכֹל אֲשֶׁר עָשָׂה לָכֶם

יהוה אֱלֹהֵיכֶם

בְּמִצְרַיִם לְעֵינֶיךָ.

וּבְאֹתוֹת —

זֶה הַמַּטֶּה,

כְּמָה שֶׁנֶּאֱמַר,

קַדֵּשׁ וּרְחַץ כַּרְפַּס יַחַץ מַגִּיד רָחְצָה מוֹצִיא מַצָּה
atzo mōtzi roch'tzo magid yachatz karpas ur'chatz kadaysh

v'es hama-te ha-ze   וְאֶת הַמַּטֶּה הַזֶּה

tikach b'yodecho   תִּקַּח בְּיָדֶךָ,

"This staff take in your hand,

asher ta-ase bō es ho-ōsōs.   אֲשֶׁר תַּעֲשֶׂה בּוֹ אֶת הָאֹתֹת.

with which you shall do the signs."

■ the first of which was Blood.

UV-MŌF'SIM.   — **וּבְמֹפְתִים**

"With wonders" —

Ze hadom.   זֶה הַדָּם,

that is the blood,

K'mo shene-emar: כְּמָה שֶׁנֶּאֱמַר,

as it says:

v'nosati mōf'sim   וְנָתַתִּי מוֹפְתִים

"I will show wonders

bashoma-yim uvo-oretz.   בַּשָּׁמַיִם וּבָאָרֶץ –

in heaven and on earth,

AS EACH OF THE WORDS דָּם, BLOOD, אֵשׁ, FIRE, AND עָשָׁן, SMOKE, IS SAID,
A BIT OF WINE IS REMOVED FROM THE CUP, WITH THE FINGER OR BY POURING.

■ This verse also alludes to the other plagues.

DOM vo-aysh v'simrōs oshon.   **דָּם** וָאֵשׁ וְתִמְרוֹת עָשָׁן.

blood and fire and pillars of smoke."

Dovor achayr   — **דָּבָר** אַחֵר

Another explanation:

b'yod chazoko sh'ta-yim.   בְּיָד חֲזָקָה, שְׁתַּיִם.

"With a mighty hand" indicates two plagues,

Uvizrō-a n'tuyo sh'ta-yim.   וּבִזְרֹעַ נְטוּיָה, שְׁתַּיִם.

"with an outstretched arm"; another two;

Uv-mōro godōl sh'ta-yim.   וּבְמֹרָא גָּדֹל, שְׁתַּיִם.

"with great fearfulness"; another two;

Uv-ōsōs sh'ta-yim.   וּבְאֹתוֹת, שְׁתַּיִם.

"with signs"; another two;

Uv-mōf'sim sh'ta-yim.   וּבְמֹפְתִים, שְׁתַּיִם.

"and with wonders"; another two —

נִרְצָה   הַלֵּל   בָּרֵךְ   צָפוּן   עוֹרֵךְ   שֻׁלְחָן   כּוֹרֵךְ   מוֹ

nirtzo   halayl   boraych   tzofun   shulchon ōraych   kōraych   mor

AYLU eser makōs   אֵלּוּ עֶשֶׂר מַכּוֹת

These are the ten plagues

shehayvi Hakodōsh boruch hu   שֶׁהֵבִיא הַקָּדוֹשׁ בָּרוּךְ הוּא

which the Holy One, Blessed is He, brought

al hamitzrim b'mitzra-yim,   עַל הַמִּצְרִים בְּמִצְרַיִם,

upon the Egyptians in Egypt,

v'aylu hayn.   וְאֵלּוּ הֵן:

and they are as follows:

AS EACH OF THE PLAGUES IS MENTIONED, A BIT OF WINE IS REMOVED FROM THE CUP.
THE SAME IS DONE BY EACH WORD OF RABBI YEHUDAH'S MNEMONIC.

■ Some wine is removed from the cup in compassion for the Egyptians.
Although they oppressed us,
we must not rejoice at the suffering of other humans.

DOM   דָּם.

Blood,

TZ'FARDAY-A   צְפַרְדֵּעַ.

Frogs,

KINIM   כִּנִּים.

Lice,

ORŌV   עָרוֹב.

Wild Beasts,

DEVER   דֶּבֶר.

Pestilence,

SH'CHIN   שְׁחִין.

Boils,

BOROD   בָּרָד.

Hail,

ARBE   אַרְבֶּה.

Locusts,

CHŌSHECH   חֹשֶׁךְ.

Darkness,

MAKAS B'CHŌRŌS.   מַכַּת בְּכוֹרוֹת.

Slaying of the Firstborn.

RABI Y'HUDO ho-yo

nōsayn bohem simonim:

רַבִּי יְהוּדָה הָיָה
נוֹתֵן בָּהֶם סִמָּנִים:

Rabbi Yehudah grouped them by their initials:

D'TZA''CH

דְּצַ''ךְ

Detzach,

ADA''SH

עֲדַ''שׁ

Adash,

B'ACHA''V.

בְּאַחַ''ב.

B'achav.

THE CUPS ARE REFILLED. THE WINE THAT WAS REMOVED IS NOT USED.

■ Scripture describes each of the Ten Plagues in detail, but all combined are but the flick of a finger compared to the blow delivered at the Sea of Reeds.

RABI YŌSAY hag'lili ōmayr.

רַבִּי יוֹסֵי הַגְּלִילִי אוֹמֵר:

Rabbi Yose the Galilean said:

Mina-yin ato ōmayr

מִנַּיִן אַתָּה אוֹמֵר

How can you come to say

sheloku hamitzrim b'mitzra-yim

שֶׁלָּקוּ הַמִּצְרִים בְּמִצְרַיִם

that the Egyptians were struck in Egypt

eser makōs

עֶשֶׂר מַכּוֹת,

by ten plagues,

v'al hayom loku

וְעַל הַיָּם לָקוּ

but at the Sea they were struck

chamishim makōs.

חֲמִשִּׁים מַכּוֹת?

by fifty plagues?

B'mitzra-yim mo hu ōmayr.

בְּמִצְרַיִם מָה הוּא אוֹמֵר,

Of the plagues in Egypt it says:

Vayōm'ru hachartumim el par-ō,

וַיֹּאמְרוּ הַחַרְטֻמִּם אֶל פַּרְעֹה,

"And the magicians said to Pharaoh,

etzba Elōhim he.

אֶצְבַּע אֱלֹהִים הוּא.

'It is the finger of God.'"

V'al ha-yom mo hu ōmayr.

וְעַל הַיָּם מָה הוּא אוֹמֵר,

Of those by the sea, however, it says:

Vayar yisro-ayl

וַיַּרְא יִשְׂרָאֵל

"When Israel saw

nirtzo   halayl   BORAYCH   tzofun   shulchon ōraych   kōraych   morō

אֶת הַיָּד הַגְּדֹלָה
es ha-yod hag'dōlo
the great hand

אֲשֶׁר עָשָׂה יהוה בְּמִצְרַיִם,
asher oso Adōnoy b'mitzra-yim
which HASHEM used in Egypt,

וַיִּרְאוּ הָעָם אֶת יהוה,
vayir'u ho-om es Adōnoy
the people feared HASHEM,

וַיַּאֲמִינוּ בַּיהוה
va-ya-aminu Ba-dōnoy
and believed in HASHEM

וּבְמֹשֶׁה עַבְדּוֹ.
uv-mōshe avdō.
and in His servant Moses.''

כַּמָּה לָקוּ בְאֶצְבַּע?
Kamo loku v'etzba
How many plagues did they receive with the finger?

עֶשֶׂר מַכּוֹת.
eser makōs.
Ten Plagues!

אֱמוֹר מֵעַתָּה,
Emōr may-ato,
Then it follows

בְּמִצְרַיִם לָקוּ עֶשֶׂר מַכּוֹת,
b'mitzra-yim loku eser makōs
that since there were ten plagues in Egypt,

וְעַל הַיָּם לָקוּ
v'al hayom loku
at the sea they were struck

חֲמִשִּׁים מַכּוֹת.
chamishim makōs.
with fifty (where they were hit with the whole hand).

■ Even the detailed account of each plague reveals but a fraction of its actual severity.

רַבִּי אֱלִיעֶזֶר אוֹמֵר.   **RABI ELI-EZER** ōmayr.
Rabbi Eliezer said:

מִנַּיִן
Mina-yin
How do we know

שֶׁכָּל מַכָּה וּמַכָּה
shekol mako umako
that each plague

שֶׁהֵבִיא הַקָּדוֹשׁ בָּרוּךְ הוּא
shehayvi Hakodōsh boruch hu
that the Holy One, Blessed is He, brought

עַל הַמִּצְרִים בְּמִצְרַיִם
al hamitzrim b'mitzra-yim
upon the Egyptians in Egypt,

קַדֵּשׁ וּרְחַץ כַּרְפַּס יַחַץ מַגִּיד רָחְצָה מוֹצִיא מַצ
kadaysh   ur'chatz   karpas   yachatz   magid   roch'tzo   mōtzi   matzo

ho-y'so shel arba makōs.   הָיְתָה שֶׁל אַרְבַּע מַכּוֹת?
consisted of four plagues?

Shene-emar: שֶׁנֶּאֱמַר,
as it says:

y'shalach bom charōn apō   — יְשַׁלַּח בָּם חֲרוֹן אַפּוֹ
"He sent forth upon them His burning anger:

evro voza-am v'tzoro   עֶבְרָה, וָזַעַם, וְצָרָה,
wrath, indignation and trouble,

mishlachas mal-achay ro-im.   מִשְׁלַחַת מַלְאֲכֵי רָעִים.
troops of messengers of evil."

Evro achas.   עֶבְרָה, אַחַת.
"Wrath" was one plague,

Voza-am sh'ta-yim.   וָזַעַם, שְׁתַּיִם.
"indignation" a second,

V'tzoro sholōsh.   וְצָרָה, שָׁלֹשׁ.
"trouble" a third

Mishlachas mal-achay ro-im arba.   מִשְׁלַחַת מַלְאֲכֵי רָעִים, אַרְבַּע.
and "troops of messengers of evil" a fourth;

Emōr may-ato   אֱמוֹר מֵעַתָּה,
consequently

b'mitzra-yim loku arbo-im makōs   בְּמִצְרַיִם לָקוּ אַרְבָּעִים מַכּוֹת,
they were struck in Egypt by forty plagues,

v'al ha-yom loku   וְעַל הַיָּם לָקוּ
and at the sea they were struck

mosa-yim makōs.   מָאתַיִם מַכּוֹת.
with two hundred plagues.

■ A deeper reading of the verses indicates that even more punishment was visited upon the Egyptians.

RABI AKIVO ōmayr.   **רַבִּי עֲקִיבָא** אוֹמֵר.
Rabbi Akiva said:

Mina-yin shekol mako umako   מִנַּיִן שֶׁכָּל מַכָּה וּמַכָּה
How do we know that each plague

nirtzo   halayl   Boraych   tzofun   shulchon ōraych   kōraych   morō

shehayvi Hakodōsh boruch hu
שֶׁהֵבִיא הַקָּדוֹשׁ בָּרוּךְ הוּא
that the Holy One, Blessed is He, brought

al hamitzrim b'mitzra-yim
עַל הַמִּצְרִים בְּמִצְרַיִם
upon the Egyptians in Egypt

ho-y'so shel chomaysh makōs.
הָיְתָה שֶׁל חָמֵשׁ מַכּוֹת?
consisted of five plagues?

Shene-emar:
שֶׁנֶּאֱמַר,
as it says:

y'shalach bom charōn apō
יְשַׁלַּח בָּם חֲרוֹן אַפּוֹ,
"He sent forth upon them His burning anger,

evro voza-am v'tzoro
עֶבְרָה, וָזַעַם, וְצָרָה,
wrath, indignation and trouble,

mishlachas mal-achay ro-im.
מִשְׁלַחַת מַלְאֲכֵי רָעִים.
troops of messengers of evil."

Charōn apō achas.
חֲרוֹן אַפּוֹ, אַחַת.
"His burning anger" was one plague,

evro sh'ta-yim.
עֶבְרָה, שְׁתַּיִם.
"wrath" a second,

Voza-am sholōsh.
וָזַעַם, שָׁלֹשׁ.
"indignation" a third,

V'tzoro arba.
וְצָרָה, אַרְבַּע.
"trouble" a fourth

Mishlachas malachay ro-im chomaysh.
מִשְׁלַחַת מַלְאֲכֵי רָעִים, חָמֵשׁ.
and "troops of messengers of evil" a fifth;

Emōr may-ato
אֱמוֹר מֵעַתָּה,
consequently

b'mitzra-yim loku
בְּמִצְרַיִם לָקוּ
they were struck in Egypt

chamishim makōs
חֲמִשִּׁים מַכּוֹת,
by fifty plagues,

v'al hayom loku
וְעַל הַיָּם לָקוּ
and at the sea they were struck

chamishim umosa-yim makōs.
חֲמִשִּׁים וּמָאתַיִם מַכּוֹת.
with two hundred and fifty plagues.

קַדֵּשׁ וּרְחַץ כַּרְפַּס יַחַץ מַגִּיד רַחְצָה מוֹצִיא מַצָּה

atzo mōtzi roch'tzo magid yachatz karpas ur'chatz kadaysh

■ In bringing us forth from slavery, God brought punishments upon our oppressors the Egyptians, their gods, their eldest and their property; He effected our physical salvation by leading us through the split Sea and catering to our physical needs; and He presented us with spiritual redemption in the form of the Sabbath, the Torah, the Holy Land and the Temple.

KAMO ma-alōs tōvōs

Lamokōm olaynu:

כַּמָה מַעֲלוֹת טוֹבוֹת
לַמָּקוֹם עָלֵינוּ:

The Ever-Present has bestowed numerous favors upon us!

Ilu hōtzi-onu mimitzra-yim

אִלוּ הוֹצִיאָנוּ מִמִּצְרַיִם

If He had brought us out of Egypt,

v'lō oso vohem sh'fotim

וְלֹא עָשָׂה בָהֶם שְׁפָטִים

but had not executed judgments upon the Egyptians,

da-yaynu.

דַּיֵּנוּ.

it would have sufficed us!

Ilu oso vohem sh'fotim

אִלוּ עָשָׂה בָהֶם שְׁפָטִים

If He had executed judgments upon them,

v'lō oso vaylōhayhem

וְלֹא עָשָׂה בֵאלֹהֵיהֶם

but not upon their gods,

da-yaynu.

דַּיֵּנוּ.

it would have sufficed for us!

Ilu oso vaylōhayhem

אִלוּ עָשָׂה בֵאלֹהֵיהֶם

If He had destroyed their gods,

v'lō horag es b'chōrayhem

וְלֹא הָרַג אֶת בְּכוֹרֵיהֶם

but not slain their firstborn,

da-yaynu.

דַּיֵּנוּ.

it would have sufficed us!

Ilu horag es b'chōrayhem

אִלוּ הָרַג אֶת בְּכוֹרֵיהֶם

If He had slain their firstborn,

v'lō nosan lonu es momōnom

וְלֹא נָתַן לָנוּ אֶת מָמוֹנָם

but not given us their wealth,

da-yaynu.

דַּיֵּנוּ.

it would have sufficed us!

Ilu nosan lonu es momōnom

אִלוּ נָתַן לָנוּ אֶת מָמוֹנָם

If He had given us their wealth,

nirtzo   halayl   boraych   tzofun   shulchon ōraych   kōraych   mor

v'lō kora lonu es ha-yom
וְלֹא קָרַע לָנוּ אֶת הַיָּם

but not split the Sea for us,

da-yaynu.
דַּיֵּנוּ.

it would have sufficed us!

Ilu kora lonu es ha-yom
אִלּוּ קָרַע לָנוּ אֶת הַיָּם

If He had split the Sea for us,

v'lō he-evironu v'sōchō
be-chorovo
וְלֹא הֶעֱבִירָנוּ בְּתוֹכוֹ
בֶּחָרָבָה

without leading us through it on dry land,

da-yaynu.
דַּיֵּנוּ.

it would have sufficed us!

Ilu he-evironu v'sōchō
bechorovo
אִלּוּ הֶעֱבִירָנוּ בְּתוֹכוֹ
בֶּחָרָבָה

If He had led us through it on dry land,

v'lō shika tzoraynu b'sōchō
וְלֹא שִׁקַּע צָרֵינוּ בְּתוֹכוֹ

but not drowned our oppressors in it,

da-yaynu.
דַּיֵּנוּ.

it would have sufficed us!

Ilu shika tzoraynu b'sōchō
אִלּוּ שִׁקַּע צָרֵינוּ בְּתוֹכוֹ

If He had drowned our oppressors in it,

v'lō sipayk tzor-kaynu bamidbor
וְלֹא סִפֵּק צָרְכֵּנוּ בַּמִּדְבָּר

but had not provided for our needs in the wilderness

arbo-im shono
אַרְבָּעִים שָׁנָה

for forty years,

da-yaynu.
דַּיֵּנוּ.

it would have sufficed us!

Ilu sipayk tzor-kaynu bamidbor
אִלּוּ סִפֵּק צָרְכֵּנוּ בַּמִּדְבָּר

If He had provided for our needs in the wilderness

arbo-im shono
אַרְבָּעִים שָׁנָה

for forty years,

v'lō he-echilonu es hamon
וְלֹא הֶאֱכִילָנוּ אֶת הַמָּן

but not fed us the manna,

da-yaynu.
דַּיֵּנוּ.

it would have sufficed us!

Ilu he-echilonu es hamon · אִלּוּ הֶאֱכִילָנוּ אֶת הַמָּן

If He had fed us the manna,

v'lō nosan lonu es hashabos · וְלֹא נָתַן לָנוּ אֶת הַשַּׁבָּת

but not given us the Sabbath,

da-yaynu. · דַּיֵּנוּ.

it would have sufficed us!

Ilu nosan lonu es hashabos · אִלּוּ נָתַן לָנוּ אֶת הַשַּׁבָּת

If He had given us the Sabbath,

v'lō kayr-vonu lifnay har sinai · וְלֹא קֵרְבָנוּ לִפְנֵי הַר סִינַי

but not brought us before Mount Sinai,

da-yaynu. · דַּיֵּנוּ.

it would have sufficed us!

Ilu kayr-vonu lifnay har sinai · אִלּוּ קֵרְבָנוּ לִפְנֵי הַר סִינַי

If He had brought us before Mount Sinai,

v'lō nosan lonu es hatōro · וְלֹא נָתַן לָנוּ אֶת הַתּוֹרָה

but not given us the Torah,

da-yaynu. · דַּיֵּנוּ.

it would have sufficed us!

Ilu nosan lonu es hatōro · אִלּוּ נָתַן לָנוּ אֶת הַתּוֹרָה

If He had given us the Torah,

v'lō hich-nisonu l'eretz yisro-ayl · וְלֹא הִכְנִיסָנוּ לְאֶרֶץ יִשְׂרָאֵל

but not brought us into the Land of Israel,

da-yaynu. · דַּיֵּנוּ.

it would have sufficed us!

Ilu hichnisonu l'eretz yisro-ayl · אִלּוּ הִכְנִיסָנוּ לְאֶרֶץ יִשְׂרָאֵל

If He had brought us into the Land of Israel,

v'lō vono lonu · וְלֹא בָנָה לָנוּ

and not built for us

es bays hab'chiro · אֶת בֵּית הַבְּחִירָה

the Temple,

da-yaynu. · דַּיֵּנוּ.

it would have sufficed us!

רור כּוֹרֵךְ שֻׁלְחָן עוֹרֵךְ צָפוּן בֵּרֵךְ הַלֵּל נִרְצָה

nirtzo · halayl · Boraych · tzofun · shulchon ōraych · kōraych · morō

■ Had God blessed us with even one of these fifteen gifts,
it would have been enough to make us immeasurably grateful.
How much more must we express our gratitude for all of them.

AL achas kamo v'chamo   עַל אַחַת כַּמָּה, וְכַמָּה

Thus, how much more so

tōvo ch'fulo um'chupeles   טוֹבָה כְפוּלָה וּמְכֻפֶּלֶת

do we owe thanks for all the manifold favors

Lamokōm olaynu.   לַמָּקוֹם עָלֵינוּ.

the Ever-Present bestowed upon us!

Shehōtzi-onu mimitzra-yim.   שֶׁהוֹצִיאָנוּ מִמִּצְרַיִם,

He brought us forth from Egypt,

V'oso vohem sh'fotim.   וְעָשָׂה בָהֶם שְׁפָטִים,

executed judgments upon them

V'oso vay-lōhayhem.   וְעָשָׂה בֵאלֹהֵיהֶם,

and upon their gods,

V'horag es b'chōrayhem.   וְהָרַג אֶת בְּכוֹרֵיהֶם,

slew their firstborn,

V'nosan lonu es momōnom.   וְנָתַן לָנוּ אֶת מָמוֹנָם,

gave us their wealth,

V'kora lonu es ha-yom.   וְקָרַע לָנוּ אֶת הַיָּם,

split the Sea for us,

V'he-evironu v'sōchō be-chorovo.   וְהֶעֱבִירָנוּ בְתוֹכוֹ בֶּחָרָבָה,

led us through it on dry land

V'shika tzoraynu b'sōchō.   וְשִׁקַּע צָרֵינוּ בְּתוֹכוֹ,

and drowned our oppressors in it,

V'sipayk tzor-kaynu bamidbor   וְסִפֵּק צָרְכֵּנוּ בַּמִּדְבָּר

provided for our needs in the wilderness

arbo-im shono.   אַרְבָּעִים שָׁנָה,

for forty years

V'he-echilonu es hamon.   וְהֶאֱכִילָנוּ אֶת הַמָּן,

and fed us the manna,

V'nosan lonu es hashabos.   וְנָתַן לָנוּ אֶת הַשַּׁבָּת,

gave us the Sabbath,

קַדֵּשׁ וּרְחַץ כַּרְפַּס יַחַץ מַגִּיד רַחְצָה מוֹצִיא מַצָּה

atzo   mōtzi   roch'tzo   **magīd**   yachatz   karpas   ur'chatz   kadaysh

V'kayr-vonu lifnay har sinai. וְקֵרְבָנוּ לִפְנֵי הַר סִינַי,

brought us before Mount Sinai,

V'nosan lonu es hatōro. וְנָתַן לָנוּ אֶת הַתּוֹרָה,

gave us the Torah,

V'hich-nisonu l'eretz yisro-ayl. וְהִכְנִיסָנוּ לְאֶרֶץ יִשְׂרָאֵל,

brought us into the Land of Israel

Uvono lonu es bays hab'chiro וּבָנָה לָנוּ אֶת בֵּית הַבְּחִירָה,

and built us a Temple

l'chapayr al kol avōnōsaynu. לְכַפֵּר עַל כָּל עֲוֹנוֹתֵינוּ.

to atone for all our sins.

■ Before singing His praise, however, we must mention the commandments of this night, and elaborate on their significance.

RABON gamli-ayl ho-yo ōmayr. רַבָּן גַּמְלִיאֵל הָיָה אוֹמֵר.

Rabban Gamliel used to say:

Kol shelō omar כָּל שֶׁלֹא אָמַר

Whoever does not explain

sh'lō-sho d'vorim aylu bapesach שְׁלֹשָׁה דְּבָרִים אֵלוּ בַּפֶּסַח,

the following three things at the Pesach festival

lō yotzo y'day chōvosō. לֹא יָצָא יְדֵי חוֹבָתוֹ,

has not fulfilled his duty,

V'aylu hayn. וְאֵלוּ הֵן,

namely:

PESACH פֶּסַח.

the Pesach sacrifice,

MATZO מַצָּה.

matzah,

UMORŌR וּמָרוֹר.

and maror.

■ The Pesach (Passover offering) recalls God's personal intervention on our behalf.

PESACH פֶּסַח

The Pesach sacrifice

sheho-yu avōsaynu ōch'lim שֶׁהָיוּ אֲבוֹתֵינוּ אוֹכְלִים

that our fathers ate

nirtzo   halayl   borаych   tzofun   shulchon ōraych   kōraych   morōr

biz-man shebays hamikdosh
ho-yo ka-yom
בִּזְמַן שֶׁבֵּית הַמִּקְדָּשׁ
הָיָה קַיָּם,

at the time when the Holy Temple was still standing —

al shum mo.
עַל שׁוּם מָה?

for what reason?

Al shum sheposach
Hakodōsh boruch hu
עַל שׁוּם שֶׁפָּסַח
הַקָּדוֹשׁ בָּרוּךְ הוּא

Because the Holy One, Blessed is He, passed over

al botay avōsaynu b'mitzra-yim.
עַל בָּתֵּי אֲבוֹתֵינוּ בְּמִצְרַיִם.

the houses of our fathers in Egypt,

Shene-emar:
שֶׁנֶּאֱמַר,

as it says:

va-amartem
וַאֲמַרְתֶּם,

"You shall say,

zevach pesach hu La-dōnoy
זֶבַח פֶּסַח הוּא לַיהוה,

it is a Pesach offering for HASHEM,

asher posach
אֲשֶׁר פָּסַח

because He passed over

al botay v'nay yisro-ayl
b'mitzra-yim
עַל בָּתֵּי בְנֵי יִשְׂרָאֵל
בְּמִצְרַיִם

the houses of the children of Israel in Egypt,

b'nog-pō es mitzra-yim
בְּנָגְפּוֹ אֶת מִצְרַיִם,

when He struck the Egyptians,

v'es botaynu hi-tzil
וְאֶת בָּתֵּינוּ הִצִּיל,

and our houses He saved;

vayikōd ho-om vayishtachavu.
וַיִּקֹּד הָעָם וַיִּשְׁתַּחֲווּ.

and the people bowed down and prostrated themselves."

THE MIDDLE MATZAH IS LIFTED AND DISPLAYED WHILE
THE FOLLOWING PARAGRAPH IS RECITED.

─────────────────────

■ The matzah alludes to the speed with which He accomplished the Exodus
when the proper time arrived.

─────────────────────

MATZO zu she-onu ōch'lim
מַצָּה זוֹ שֶׁאָנוּ אוֹכְלִים,

This matzah that we eat —

קַדֵּשׁ וּרְחַץ כַּרְפַּס יַחַץ מַגִּיד רָחְצָה מוֹצִיא מַ...

atzo   mōtzi   rōch'tzo   magid   yachatz   karpas   ur'chatz   kadaysh

al shum mo. עַל שׁוּם מָה?

for what reason?

Al shum עַל שׁוּם

Because

shelō hispik b'tzaykom שֶׁלֹא הִסְפִּיק בְּצֵקָם

shel avōsaynu l'hachamitz שֶׁל אֲבוֹתֵינוּ לְהַחֲמִיץ,

the dough of our fathers did not have time to become leavened

ad sheniglo alayhem עַד שֶׁנִּגְלָה עֲלֵיהֶם

melech malchay ham'lochim מֶלֶךְ מַלְכֵי הַמְּלָכִים

Hakodōsh boruch hu הַקָּדוֹשׁ בָּרוּךְ הוּא

before the King of kings, the Holy One, Blessed is He, revealed Himself to them

ug-olom. וּגְאָלָם.

and redeemed them;

Shene-emar: שֶׁנֶּאֱמַר,

as it says:

vayōfu es habo-tzayk וַיֹּאפוּ אֶת הַבָּצֵק

"And they baked the dough,

asher hōtzi-u mimitzra-yim אֲשֶׁר הוֹצִיאוּ מִמִּצְרַיִם

which they had taken with them from Egypt,

ugōs matzōs עֻגֹת מַצּוֹת

into unleavened bread

ki lō chomaytz כִּי לֹא חָמֵץ,

for it was not leavened,

ki gōr'shu mimitzra-yim כִּי גֹרְשׁוּ מִמִּצְרַיִם,

because they were driven out of Egypt

v'lō yoch'lu l'hismahmayha וְלֹא יָכְלוּ לְהִתְמַהְמֵהַּ,

and could not delay there;

v'gam tzaydo lō osu lohem. וְגַם צֵדָה לֹא עָשׂוּ לָהֶם.

nor had they prepared for themselves any provisions for the way."

THE MAROR IS LIFTED AND DISPLAYED WHILE THE FOLLOWING PARAGRAPH IS RECITED.

■ And the maror (bitter herbs) symbolizes our bitter lot under the Egyptians.

MORŌR ze she-onu ōch'lim מָרוֹר זֶה שֶׁאָנוּ אוֹכְלִים,

This maror that we eat —

nirtzo halayl borach tzofun shulchon ōrach kōrach mor

al shum mo.

עַל שׁוּם מָה?

for what reason?

Al shum shemayr'ru hamitzrim

עַל שׁוּם שֶׁמֵּרְרוּ הַמִּצְרִים

Because the Egyptians embittered

es cha-yay avōsaynu b'mitzra-yim.

אֶת חַיֵּי אֲבוֹתֵינוּ בְּמִצְרָיִם.

the lives of our fathers in Egypt;

Shene-emar:

שֶׁנֶּאֱמַר,

as it says:

vai-mor'ru es cha-yayhem

וַיְמָרְרוּ אֶת חַיֵּיהֶם,

"They made their lives bitter

ba-avōdo kosho

בַּעֲבֹדָה קָשָׁה,

with hard labor,

b'chōmer uvilvaynim

בְּחֹמֶר וּבִלְבֵנִים,

with mortar and with bricks,

uv-chol avōdo basode

וּבְכָל עֲבֹדָה בַּשָּׂדֶה,

and through all manner of labor in the field;

ays kol avōdosom

אֵת כָּל עֲבֹדָתָם

all their labors

asher ov'du vohem b'forech.

אֲשֶׁר עָבְדוּ בָהֶם בְּפָרֶךְ.

that they performed for them were with crushing harshness."

■ The memorials of the night must evoke a feeling of personal relief from suffering.
Not only our ancestors, but also we were redeemed.
We should feel as though we too were slaves and then redeemed.

B'CHOL DŌR VODŌR

בְּכָל דּוֹר וָדוֹר

In every generation,

cha-yov odom lir-ōs es atzmo

חַיָּב אָדָם לִרְאוֹת אֶת עַצְמוֹ

one is obliged to regard himself

k'ilu hu yotzo mimitzra-yim.

כְּאִלּוּ הוּא יָצָא מִמִּצְרָיִם.

as though he himself had actually gone out from Egypt,

Shene-emar:

שֶׁנֶּאֱמַר,

as it says:

v'higad-to l'vincho ba-yōm hahu
lay-mōr:

וְהִגַּדְתָּ לְבִנְךָ בַּיּוֹם הַהוּא
לֵאמֹר,

"You shall tell your son on that day, saying:

tzo   mōtzi   roch'tzo   magid   yachatz   karpas   ur'chatz   kadaysh   קַדֵּשׁ וּרְחַץ כַּרְפַּס יַחַץ מַגִּיד רָחְצָה מוֹצִיא מַצָּ

ba-avur ze oso Adōnoy li   בַּעֲבוּר זֶה עָשָׂה יהוה לִי,
'For the sake of this, HASHEM did so for me

b'tzaysi mimitzro-yim.   בְּצֵאתִי מִמִּצְרָיִם.
when I went out from Egypt.'"

Lō es avōsaynu bilvod   לֹא אֶת אֲבוֹתֵינוּ בִּלְבָד
Not only our fathers

go-al Hakodōsh boruch hu   גָּאַל הַקָּדוֹשׁ בָּרוּךְ הוּא,
did the Holy One, Blessed is He, redeem,

elo af ōsonu go-al imohem.   אֶלָּא אַף אוֹתָנוּ גָּאַל עִמָּהֶם.
but also us did He redeem with them,

Shene-emar: שֶׁנֶּאֱמַר,
as it says:

v'ōsonu hōtzi mishom   וְאוֹתָנוּ הוֹצִיא מִשָּׁם,
"And He brought 'us' out from there,

l'ma-an hovi ōsonu   לְמַעַן הָבִיא אֹתָנוּ
so that He might bring us

loses lonu es ho-oretz   לָתֶת לָנוּ אֶת הָאָרֶץ
and give us the land

asher nishba la-avōsaynu.   אֲשֶׁר נִשְׁבַּע לַאֲבוֹתֵינוּ.
which He had promised to our fathers."

THE MATZOS ARE COVERED AND THE CUP IS LIFTED AND HELD UNTIL IT IS TO BE DRUNK. ACCORDING TO SOME CUSTOMS, HOWEVER, THE CUP IS PUT DOWN AFTER THE FOLLOWING PARAGRAPH, IN WHICH CASE THE MATZOS SHOULD ONCE MORE BE UNCOVERED. IF THIS CUSTOM IS FOLLOWED, THE MATZOS ARE TO BE COVERED AND THE CUP RAISED AGAIN UPON REACHING THE BLESSING אֲשֶׁר גְּאָלָנוּ, WHO HAS REDEEMED US (BOTTOM OF PAGE 70).

■ Therefore, we must offer thanks. For the many manifestations
of our redemption, we shall now sing God's praises.

L'FICHOCH anachnu cha-yovim   לְפִיכָךְ אֲנַחְנוּ חַיָּבִים
Therefore it is our duty

l'hōdōs l'halayl l'shabay-ach   לְהוֹדוֹת, לְהַלֵּל, לְשַׁבֵּחַ,
to thank, to praise, to laud,

l'fo-ayr l'rōmaym l'hadayr   לְפָאֵר, לְרוֹמֵם, לְהַדֵּר,
to glorify, to exalt, to honor,

l'voraych l'alay ul'kalays   לְבָרֵךְ, לְעַלֵּה, וּלְקַלֵּס,
to bless, to extol and acclaim

מור   kōraych   shulchon ōraych   tzofun   вoraych   halayl   nirtzo

l'mi she-oso la-avōsaynu v'lonu   לְמִי שֶׁעָשָׂה לַאֲבוֹתֵינוּ וְלָנוּ
the One Who performed for our fathers and for us

es kol hanisim ho-aylu.   אֶת כָּל הַנִּסִּים הָאֵלּוּ,
all these miracles.

Hōtzi-onu may-avdus l'chayrus,   הוֹצִיאָנוּ מֵעַבְדוּת לְחֵרוּת,
He has brought us forth from slavery to freedom,

mi-yogōn l'simcho,   מִיָּגוֹן לְשִׂמְחָה,
from sorrow to joy,

umay-ayvel l'yōm tōv,   וּמֵאֵבֶל לְיוֹם טוֹב,
from mourning to festivity,

umay-afaylo l'ōr godōl,   וּמֵאֲפֵלָה לְאוֹר גָּדוֹל,
from darkness to bright light,

umishibud lig-ulo,   וּמִשִּׁעְבּוּד לִגְאֻלָּה,
and from bondage to redemption.

v'nōmar l'fonov shiro chadosho   וְנֹאמַר לְפָנָיו שִׁירָה חֲדָשָׁה,
Therefore let us recite a new song before Him.

hal'luyoh.   הַלְלוּיָהּ.
Hallelujah!

■ We are no longer Pharaoh's slaves; our obligations are solely to the One Who elevated us from our lowly stature in Egypt and endowed us with nobility.

HAL'LUYOH,   הַלְלוּיָהּ
Praise God!

hal'lu avday Adōnoy,   הַלְלוּ עַבְדֵי יהוה,
Give praise, you servants of HASHEM;

hal'lu es shaym Adōnoy.   הַלְלוּ אֶת שֵׁם יהוה.
praise the Name of HASHEM!

Y'hi shaym Adōnoy m'vōroch,   יְהִי שֵׁם יהוה מְבֹרָךְ,
Blessed be the Name of HASHEM,

may-ato v'ad ōlom.   מֵעַתָּה וְעַד עוֹלָם.
from this time and forever.

Mimizrach shemesh ad m'vō-ō,   מִמִּזְרַח שֶׁמֶשׁ עַד מְבוֹאוֹ,
From the rising of the sun to its setting,

m'hulol shaym Adōnoy.   מְהֻלָּל שֵׁם יהוה.
HASHEM's Name is praised.

Rom al kol gōyim Adōnoy, רָם עַל כָּל גּוֹיִם יהוה,
High above all nations is HASHEM,

al ha-shoma-yim k'vōdō. עַל הַשָּׁמַיִם כְּבוֹדוֹ.
above the heavens is His glory.

Mi Ka-dōnoy Elōhaynu, מִי כַּיהוה אֱלֹהֵינוּ,
Who is like HASHEM, our God,

hamagbihi lo-shoves. הַמַּגְבִּיהִי לָשָׁבֶת.
Who is enthroned on high —

Hamashpili lir-ōs, הַמַּשְׁפִּילִי לִרְאוֹת,
yet Who lowers Himself to look

ba-shoma-yim u-vo-oretz. בַּשָּׁמַיִם וּבָאָרֶץ.
upon the heaven and the earth?

M'kimi may-ofor dol, מְקִימִי מֵעָפָר דָּל,
He raises the destitiute from the dust,

may-ashpōs yorim evyōn. מֵאַשְׁפֹּת יָרִים אֶבְיוֹן.
from the trash heaps He lifts the needy.

L'hōshivi im n'divim, לְהוֹשִׁיבִי עִם נְדִיבִים,
im n'divay amō. עִם נְדִיבֵי עַמּוֹ.
To seat them with nobles, with the nobles of His people.

Mōshivi akeres haba-yis, מוֹשִׁיבִי עֲקֶרֶת הַבַּיִת,
He transforms the barren wife

aym habonim s'maycho, אֵם הַבָּנִים שְׂמֵחָה,
into a glad mother of children.

hal'luyoh. הַלְלוּיָהּ.
Praise God!

■ The laws of nature were subverted during the Exodus. Sea and mountain fled to allow God and His nation to pass.

B'TZAYS yisro-ayl mimitzro-yim, בְּצֵאת יִשְׂרָאֵל מִמִּצְרָיִם,
When Israel went out of Egypt,

bays ya-akōv may-am lō-ayz. בֵּית יַעֲקֹב מֵעַם לֹעֵז.
Jacob's household from a people of alien tongue —

Hoy'so y'hudo l'kod-shō, הָיְתָה יְהוּדָה לְקָדְשׁוֹ,
Judah became His sanctuary,

yisro-ayl mamsh'lōsov.

יִשְׂרָאֵל מַמְשְׁלוֹתָיו.

Israel His dominions.

Ha-yom ro-o va-yonōs,

הַיָּם רָאָה וַיָּנֹס,

The sea saw and fled:

ha-yardayn yisōv l'ochōr.

הַיַּרְדֵּן יִסֹּב לְאָחוֹר.

the Jordan turned backward.

Hehorim rok'du ch'aylim,

הֶהָרִים רָקְדוּ כְאֵילִים,

The mountains skipped like rams,

g'vo-ōs kivnay tzōn.

גְּבָעוֹת כִּבְנֵי צֹאן.

the hills like young lambs.

Ma l'cho ha-yom ki sonus,

מַה לְּךָ הַיָּם כִּי תָנוּס,

What ails you, O sea, that you flee?

ha-yardayn tisōv l'ochōr.

הַיַּרְדֵּן תִּסֹּב לְאָחוֹר.

O Jordan, that you turn backward?

Hehorim tirk'du ch'aylim,

הֶהָרִים תִּרְקְדוּ כְאֵילִים,

O mountains, that you skip like rams?

g'vo-ōs kivnay tzōn.

גְּבָעוֹת כִּבְנֵי צֹאן.

O hills, like young lambs?

Milifnay odōn chuli oretz,

מִלִּפְנֵי אָדוֹן חוּלִי אָרֶץ,

Before the Lord's Presence, tremble, O earth,

milifnay Elō-a ya-akōv.

מִלִּפְנֵי אֱלוֹהַּ יַעֲקֹב.

before the presence of the God of Jacob,

Hahōf'chi hatzur agam mo-yim,

הַהֹפְכִי הַצּוּר אֲגַם מָיִם,

Who turns the rock into a pond of water,

chalomish l'ma-y'nō mo-yim.

חַלָּמִישׁ לְמַעְיְנוֹ מָיִם.

the flint into a flowing fountain.

ACCORDING TO ALL CUSTOMS THE CUP IS LIFTED AND THE MATZOHS COVERED
DURING THE RECITATION OF THIS BLESSING.

■ The Exodus was not an end unto itself, but a prelude to our entry into the Holy Land and the erection of the Temple in Jerusalem. Thus, the formal thanksgiving blessing for the redemption includes a prayer for a rebuilt Temple and the resumption of our worship there.

BORUCH ato Adōnoy

בָּרוּךְ אַתָּה יהוה

Blessed are You, HASHEM,

קַדֵּשׁ וּרְחַץ כַּרְפַּס יַחַץ מַגִּיד רָחְצָה מוֹצִיא מַצָּה

atzo   mōtzi   roch'tzo   magid   yachatz   karpas   ur'chatz   kadaysh

Elōhaynu melech ho-ōlom

אֱלֹהֵינוּ מֶלֶךְ הָעוֹלָם,

our God, King of the universe,

asher g'olonu

אֲשֶׁר גְּאָלָנוּ

Who redeemed us

v'go-al es avōsaynu

וְגָאַל אֶת אֲבוֹתֵינוּ

and redeemed our fathers

mimitzra-yim

מִמִּצְרַיִם,

from Egypt

v'higi-onu halai-lo ha-ze

וְהִגִּיעָנוּ הַלַּיְלָה הַזֶּה

and brought us, on this night,

le-echol bō matzo umorōr.

לֶאֱכָל בּוֹ מַצָּה וּמָרוֹר.

to eat on it matzah and maror.

Kayn Adōnoy Elōhaynu

כֵּן יהוה אֱלֹהֵינוּ

Vay-lōhay avōsaynu

וֵאלֹהֵי אֲבוֹתֵינוּ,

Thus may HASHEM, our God and God of our fathers,

yagi-aynu

יַגִּיעֵנוּ

bring us

l'mō-adim v'lirgolim achayrim

לְמוֹעֲדִים וְלִרְגָלִים אֲחֵרִים

to future festivals and holidays

habo-im likrosaynu l'sholōm

הַבָּאִים לִקְרָאתֵנוּ לְשָׁלוֹם,

that may come to us in peace,

s'maychim b'vinyan irecho

שְׂמֵחִים בְּבִנְיַן עִירֶךָ

when we shall rejoice in the rebuilding of Your city

v'sosim ba-avōdosecho.

וְשָׂשִׂים בַּעֲבוֹדָתֶךָ,

and shall be joyful in Your Temple service;

v'nōchal shom

וְנֹאכַל שָׁם

and there we shall partake

min haz'vochim umin hap'sochim

מִן הַזְּבָחִים וּמִן הַפְּסָחִים

of the sacrifices and the Pesach offerings

ON SATURDAY NIGHT, SAY THIS IN PLACE OF THE PREVIOUS LINE:

min hap'sochim umin haz'vochim

מִן הַפְּסָחִים וּמִן הַזְּבָחִים

of the Pesach offerings and the sacrifices

asher yagi-a domom

אֲשֶׁר יַגִּיעַ דָּמָם

whose blood will be sprinkled

רחץ כּוֹרֵךְ שֻׁלְחָן עוֹרֵךְ צָפוּן בָּרֵךְ הַלֵּל נִרְצָה

nirtzo   halayl   boraych   tzofun   shulchon ōraych   kōraych   mor

al kir mizbachacho

עַל קִיר מִזְבַּחֲךָ

upon the sides of Your Altar

l'rotzōn

לְרָצוֹן.

for gracious acceptance.

V'nōde l'cho shir chodosh

וְנוֹדֶה לְךָ שִׁיר חָדָשׁ

Then we shall thank You with a new song

al g'ulosaynu

עַל גְּאֻלָּתֵנוּ

for our redemption

v'al p'dus nafshaynu.

וְעַל פְּדוּת נַפְשֵׁנוּ.

and for the deliverance of our souls.

Boruch ato Adōnoy

בָּרוּךְ אַתָּה יהוה,

Blessed are You, HASHEM,

go-al yisro-ayl.

גָּאַל יִשְׂרָאֵל.

Who has redeemed Israel.

BORUCH ato Adōnoy

בָּרוּךְ אַתָּה יהוה

Blessed are You, HASHEM,

Elōhaynu melech ho-ōlom

אֱלֹהֵינוּ מֶלֶךְ הָעוֹלָם,

our God, King of the universe,

bōray p'ri hagofen.

בּוֹרֵא פְּרִי הַגָּפֶן.

Who creates the fruit of the vine.

THE SECOND CUP IS DRUNK WHILE LEANING ON THE LEFT SIDE —
PREFERABLY THE ENTIRE CUP IS DRAINED, BUT AT THE VERY LEAST MOST OF IT.

✌ רחצה / **RACHTZO**

WASH THE HANDS. THE HANDS ARE WASHED FOR MATZAH AND THE FOLLOWING BLESSING IS RECITED. IT IS PREFERABLE TO BRING WATER AND A BASIN TO THE HEAD OF THE HOUSE-HOLD AT THE SEDER TABLE.

BORUCH ato Adōnoy

בָּרוּךְ אַתָּה יהוה

Blessed are You, HASHEM,

Elōhaynu melech ho-ōlom

אֱלֹהֵינוּ מֶלֶךְ הָעוֹלָם,

our God, King of the universe,

asher kid'shonu b'mitzvōsov

אֲשֶׁר קִדְּשָׁנוּ בְּמִצְוֹתָיו,

Who has sanctified us by His commandments

v'tzivonu al n'tilas yodo-yim.

וְצִוָּנוּ עַל נְטִילַת יָדָיִם.

and has commanded us concerning the washing of the hands.

קַדֵּשׁ וּרְחַץ כַּרְפַּס יַחַץ מַגִּיד רָחְצָה מוֹצִיא מַ
tzo mōtzi roch'tzo magid yachatz karpas ur'chatz kadaysh

מוֹצִיא / MOTZI

THE FOLLOWING TWO BLESSINGS ARE RECITED OVER MATZAH; THE FIRST IS RECITED OVER
MATZAH AS FOOD, AND THE SECOND FOR THE SPECIAL MITZVAH OF EATING MATZAH ON THE
NIGHT OF PASSOVER. [THE LATTER BLESSING IS TO BE MADE WITH THE INTENTION THAT IT
ALSO APPLY TO THE "SANDWICH" AND THE AFIKOMAN.]

THE HEAD OF THE HOUSEHOLD RAISES ALL THE MATZOS ON THE SEDER PLATE
AND RECITES THE FOLLOWING BLESSING:

■ The blessing over matzah as food, as the more common benediction, is recited first.

BORUCH ato Adōnoy   בָּרוּךְ אַתָּה יהוה

Blessed are You, HASHEM,

Elōhaynu melech ho-ōlom   אֱלֹהֵינוּ מֶלֶךְ הָעוֹלָם,

our God, King of the universe,

hamōtzi lechem min ho-oretz.   הַמּוֹצִיא לֶחֶם מִן הָאָרֶץ.

Who brings forth bread from the earth.

THE BOTTOM MATZAH IS PUT DOWN AND THE FOLLOWING BLESSING IS RECITED WHILE
THE TOP (WHOLE) MATZAH AND THE MIDDLE (BROKEN) PIECE ARE STILL RAISED.

מַצָּה / MATZO

■ The matzah of Pesach is no mere substitute for bread, however. Its use is in
fulfillment of a commandment, and it therefore requires a blessing of its own.

BORUCH ato Adōnoy   בָּרוּךְ אַתָּה יהוה

Blessed are You, HASHEM,

Elōhaynu melech ho-ōlom   אֱלֹהֵינוּ מֶלֶךְ הָעוֹלָם,

our God, King of the universe,

asher kid'shonu b'mitzvōsov   אֲשֶׁר קִדְּשָׁנוּ בְּמִצְוֹתָיו,

Who has sanctified us by His commandments

v'tzivonu al achilas matzo.   וְצִוָּנוּ עַל אֲכִילַת מַצָּה.

and has commanded us concerning the eating of matzah.

EACH PARTICIPANT IS REQUIRED TO EAT AN AMOUNT OF MATZAH EQUAL IN VOLUME TO AN
EGG. SINCE IT IS IMPOSSIBLE TO PROVIDE A SUFFICIENT AMOUNT OF MATZAH FROM THE TWO
MATZOS FOR ALL MEMBERS OF THE HOUSEHOLD, OTHER MATZOS SHOULD BE AVAILABLE
AT THE TABLE FROM WHICH TO COMPLETE THE REQUIRED AMOUNTS. HOWEVER, EACH PAR-
TICIPANT SHOULD RECEIVE A PIECE FROM EACH OF THE TOP TWO MATZOS.

THE MATZOS ARE TO BE EATEN WHILE RECLINING ON THE LEFT SIDE
AND WITHOUT DELAY; THEY NEED NOT BE DIPPED IN SALT.

nirtzo   halayl   Boraych   tzofun   shulchon ōraych   kōraych   morō

✌ מרור / MOROR

THE HEAD OF THE HOUSEHOLD TAKES A HALF-EGG VOLUME OF MAROR, DIPS IT INTO
CHAROSES, SHAKES OFF THE CHAROSES AND GIVES EACH PARTICIPANT A LIKE AMOUNT.

THE FOLLOWING BLESSING IS RECITED WITH THE INTENTION
THAT IT ALSO APPLY TO THE MAROR OF THE "SANDWICH."

THE MAROR IS EATEN WITHOUT RECLINING, AND WITHOUT DELAY.

■ The maror symbolizes the bitterness inflicted by the Egyptians. Charoses (literally,
potter's clay) resembles the mortar with which our ancestors built Egyptian cities.
Additionally, the apple, nuts, cinnamon and other ingredients of the charoses are
used in Song of Songs as symbols of the qualities of the Jewish people.

BORUCH ato Adōnoy   בָּרוּךְ אַתָּה יהוה

Blessed are You, HASHEM,

Elōhaynu melech ho-ōlom   אֱלֹהֵינוּ מֶלֶךְ הָעוֹלָם,

our God, King of the universe,

asher kid'shonu b'mitzvōsov   אֲשֶׁר קִדְּשָׁנוּ בְּמִצְוֹתָיו,

Who has sanctified us by His commandments

v'tzivonu al achilas morōr.   וְצִוָּנוּ עַל אֲכִילַת מָרוֹר.

and has commanded us concerning the eating of maror.

✌ כורך /KŌRAYCH

THE BOTTOM (THUS FAR UNBROKEN) MATZAH IS NOW TAKEN.
FROM IT, WITH THE ADDITION OF OTHER MATZOS, EACH PARTICIPANT RECEIVES A HALF-EGG
VOLUME OF MATZAH ALONG WITH AN EQUAL-VOLUME PORTION OF MAROR (DIPPED
INTO CHAROSES WHICH IS SHAKEN OFF). THE FOLLOWING PARAGRAPH IS RECITED AND THE
"SANDWICH" IS EATEN WHILE RECLINING.

ZAYCHER l'mikdosh k'hilayl.   זֵכֶר לְמִקְדָּשׁ כְּהִלֵּל.

In remembrance of the Temple we do as Hillel did.

Kayn oso hilayl   כֵּן עָשָׂה הִלֵּל

This is what Hillel did

bizman shebays hamikdosh   בִּזְמַן שֶׁבֵּית הַמִּקְדָּשׁ
ho-yo ka-yom.   הָיָה קַיָּם.

in Temple times:

Ho-yo kōraych (Pesach)   הָיָה כּוֹרֵךְ (פֶּסַח)
matzo umorōr   מַצָּה וּמָרוֹר

He would combine (the Pesach offering,) matzah and maror in a sandwich

קַדֵּשׁ וּרְחַץ כַּרְפַּס יַחַץ מַגִּיד רָחְצָה מוֹצִיא מַצָּ

matzo   mōtzi   roch'tzo   magid   yachatz   karpas   ur'chatz   kadaysh v'ōchayl b'yachad

וְאוֹכֵל בְּיַחַד.

and eat them together,

l'ka-yaym ma shene-emar

לְקַיֵּם מַה שֶׁנֶּאֱמַר,

to fulfill what it says:

al matzōs um'rōrim yōchluhu.

עַל מַצּוֹת וּמְרֹרִים יֹאכְלֻהוּ.

They shall eat it with matzos and bitter herbs.

✒ שלחן עורך /SHULCHON ŌRAYCH

THE MEAL SHOULD BE EATEN IN A COMBINATION OF JOY AND SOLEMNITY, FOR THE MEAL, TOO, IS PART OF THE SEDER SERVICE. WHILE IT IS DESIRABLE THAT ZEMIROS AND DISCUSSION OF THE LAWS AND EVENTS OF PASSOVER BE PART OF THE MEAL, EXTRANEOUS CONVERSATION SHOULD BE AVOIDED. IT SHOULD BE REMEMBERED THAT THE AFIKOMAN MUST BE EATEN WHILE THERE IS STILL SOME APPETITE FOR IT. IN FACT, IF ONE IS SO SATED THAT HE MUST LITERALLY FORCE HIMSELF TO EAT IT, HE IS NOT CREDITED WITH THE PERFORMANCE OF THE MITZVAH OF AFIKOMAN. THEREFORE, IT IS UNWISE TO EAT MORE THAN A MODERATE AMOUNT DURING THE MEAL.

✒ צפון /TZOFUN

■ We allow the taste of the afikoman ("dessert") to linger in our mouths; for the afikoman — a piece of bland matzah — signifies that it is not the sweetness of the food which whets our palate, but the observance of mitzvos which is "sweeter than honey dripping from the combs."

FROM THE AFIKOMAN MATZAH (AND FROM ADDITIONAL MATZOS TO MAKE UP THE RE-QUIRED AMOUNT) A HALF-EGG VOLUME PORTION — ACCORDING TO SOME, A FULL EGG VOLUME PORTION — IS GIVEN TO EACH PARTICIPANT. IT SHOULD BE EATEN BEFORE MID-NIGHT, WHILE RECLINING, WITHOUT DELAY, AND UNINTERRUPTEDLY. EXCEPT FOR THE LAST TWO SEDER CUPS OF WINE, NOTHING MAY BE EATEN OR DRUNK AFTER THE AFIKOMAN (WITH THE EXCEPTION OF WATER AND THE LIKE).

✒ ברך / BORAYCH

THE THIRD CUP IS POURED AND BIRCAS HAMAZON (GRACE AFTER MEALS) IS RECITED. ACCORDING TO SOME CUSTOMS, THE CUP OF ELIJAH IS POURED AT THIS POINT.

■ On all festive days the Grace is prefaced with Psalm 126 which describes the joys of redemption.

SHIR hama-alōs,

שִׁיר הַמַּעֲלוֹת,

A song of ascents.

b'shuv Adōnoy

בְּשׁוּב יהוה

es shivas tziyōn,

אֶת שִׁיבַת צִיּוֹן,

When HASHEM will return the captives of Zion,

ho-yinu k'chōl'mim.   הָיִינוּ כְּחֹלְמִים.
we will be like dreamers.

Oz yimolay s'chōk pinu   אָז יִמָּלֵא שְׂחוֹק פִּינוּ
Then our mouth will be filled with laughter

ulshōnaynu rino,   וּלְשׁוֹנֵנוּ רִנָּה,
and our tongue with glad song.

oz yōm'ru vagōyim,   אָז יֹאמְרוּ בַגּוֹיִם,
Then they will declare among the nations,

higdil Adōnoy la-asōs im ayle.   הִגְדִּיל יהוה לַעֲשׂוֹת עִם אֵלֶּה.
"HASHEM has done greatly with these."

Higdil Adōnoy la-asōs imonu   הִגְדִּיל יהוה לַעֲשׂוֹת עִמָּנוּ,
HASHEM has done greatly with us,

ho-yinu s'maychim.   הָיִינוּ שְׂמֵחִים.
we were gladdened.

Shuvo Adōnoy es sh'visaynu   שׁוּבָה יהוה אֶת שְׁבִיתֵנוּ,
O HASHEM — return our captivity

ka-afikim banegev.   כַּאֲפִיקִים בַּנֶּגֶב.
like springs in the desert.

Hazōr'im b'dim-o   הַזֹּרְעִים בְּדִמְעָה
Those who tearfully sow

b'rino yiktzōru.   בְּרִנָּה יִקְצֹרוּ.
will reap in glad song.

Holōch yaylaych uvochō   הָלוֹךְ יֵלֵךְ וּבָכֹה
He walks along weeping,

nōsay meshech hazora,   נֹשֵׂא מֶשֶׁךְ הַזָּרַע,
he who bears the measure of seeds,

bō yovō v'rino, nōsay alumōsov.   בֹּא יָבֹא בְרִנָּה, נֹשֵׂא אֲלֻמֹּתָיו.
but will return in exultation, a bearer of his sheaves.

T'HILAS Adonoy y'daber pi,   **תְּהִלַּת** יהוה יְדַבֶּר פִּי,
May my mouth declare the praise of HASHEM

vivoraych kol bosor   וִיבָרֵךְ כָּל בָּשָׂר
shem kodshō l'ōlom vo-ed.   שֵׁם קָדְשׁוֹ לְעוֹלָם וָעֶד.
and may all flesh bless His Holy Name forever.

קַדֵּשׁ וּרְחַץ כַּרְפַּס יַחַץ מַגִּיד רָחְצָה מוֹצִיא מַצָ
atzo   mōtzi   roch'tzo   magid   yachatz   karpas   ur'chatz   kadaysh

Va-anachnu n'voraych Yoh,　　　　　　　וַאֲנַחְנוּ נְבָרֵךְ יָהּ,

We will bless HASHEM

may-ato v'ad ōlam, hal'luyoh.　　　מֵעַתָּה וְעַד עוֹלָם, הַלְלוּיָהּ.

from this time and forever, Praise God!

Hōdu La-dōnoy ki tōv,　　　　　　　הוֹדוּ לַיהוה כִּי טוֹב,

Give thanks to God for He is good,

ki l'ōlom chasdō.　　　　　　　　　כִּי לְעוֹלָם חַסְדּוֹ.

for His kindness endures forever.

Mi y'malayl g'vurōs Adōnoy,　　　　מִי יְמַלֵּל גְּבוּרוֹת יהוה,

Who can express the mighty acts of HASHEM?

yashmi-a kol t'hilosō.　　　　　　יַשְׁמִיעַ כָּל תְּהִלָּתוֹ.

Who can declare all His praise?

Hin'ni muchon umzumōn　　　　　　הִנְנִי מוּכָן וּמְזֻמָּן

Behold I am prepared and ready

l'ka-yaym mitzvas asay　　　　　לְקַיֵּם מִצְוַת עֲשֵׂה

to perform the positive commandment

shel birkas hamozōn,　　　　　　שֶׁל בִּרְכַּת הַמָּזוֹן,

of Grace After Meals,

shene-emar:　　　　　　　　　　שֶׁנֶּאֱמַר:

as it says:

v'ochalto v'sovoto,　　　　　　וְאָכַלְתָּ וְשָׂבָעְתָּ,

"And you shall eat and you shall be satisfied

u-vayrachto es Adōnoy Elōhecho,　וּבֵרַכְתָּ אֶת יהוה אֱלֹהֶיךָ,

and you shall bless HASHEM, your God,

al ho-oretz hatōvo　　　　　　　עַל הָאָרֶץ הַטֹּבָה

　asher nosan loch.　　　　　　אֲשֶׁר נָתַן לָךְ.

for the good land which He gave you."

IF THREE OR MORE MALES, AGED THIRTEEN OR OLDER, PARTICIPATE IN A MEAL, A LEADER IS APPOINTED TO FORMALLY INVITE THE OTHERS TO JOIN HIM IN RECITING GRACE AFTER MEALS. FOLLOWING IS THE "ZIMUN," OR FORMAL INVITATION.

■ The Psalmist called to his people, "Declare the greatness of Hashem with me, and let us exalt His Name together!" Accordingly the Sages ordained that when three eat together, one of them should declare God's greatness, and the others respond together in praise of His Name.

nirtzo　　holayl　BORaych　tzofun　shulchon ōraych　kōraych　morōr

THE LEADER BEGINS:

RABŌSAI n'voraych.

רַבּוֹתַי נְבָרֵךְ.

Gentlemen, let us bless.

THE GROUP RESPONDS:

Y'hi shaym Adōnoy m'vōroch

יְהִי שֵׁם יהוה מְבֹרָךְ

Blessed be the Name of HASHEM

may-ato v'ad ōlom.

מֵעַתָּה וְעַד עוֹלָם.

from this time and forever!

THE LEADER CONTINUES:

Y'hi shaym Adōnoy m'vōroch

יְהִי שֵׁם יהוה מְבֹרָךְ

Blessed be the Name of HASHEM

may-ato v'ad ōlom.

מֵעַתָּה וְעַד עוֹלָם.

from this time and forever!

IF TEN MEN JOIN IN THE *ZIMUN*, אֱלֹהֵינוּ, *OUR GOD,* IS ADDED.

Bir-shus moronon v'rabonon
v'rabōsai,

בִּרְשׁוּת מָרָנָן וְרַבָּנָן
וְרַבּוֹתַי,

With the permission of my masters, rabbis and teachers,

n'voraych (Elōhaynu)
she-ochalnu mi-shelō.

נְבָרֵךְ (אֱלֹהֵינוּ)
שֶׁאָכַלְנוּ מִשֶּׁלּוֹ.

let us bless [our God,] He of Whose we have eaten.

THE GROUP RESPONDS:

Boruch (Elōhaynu)
she-ochalnu mi-shelō

בָּרוּךְ (אֱלֹהֵינוּ)
שֶׁאָכַלְנוּ מִשֶּׁלּוֹ

Blessed is [our God,] He of Whose we have eaten

uvtuvō cho-yinu.

וּבְטוּבוֹ חָיִינוּ.

and through Whose goodness we live.

THE LEADER CONTINUES:

Boruch (Elōhaynu)
she-ochalnu mishelō

בָּרוּךְ (אֱלֹהֵינוּ)
שֶׁאָכַלְנוּ מִשֶּׁלּוֹ

Blessed is [our God,] He of Whose we have eaten

uvtuvō cho-yinu.

וּבְטוּבוֹ חָיִינוּ.

and through Whose goodness we live.

THE FOLLOWING LINE IS RECITED IF TEN MEN JOIN IN THE ZIMUN:

Boruch hu uvoruch sh'mō.

בָּרוּךְ הוּא וּבָרוּךְ שְׁמוֹ.

Blessed is He and Blessed is His Name.

atzo   mōtzi   roch'tzo   magid   yachatz   karpas   ur'chatz   kadaysh

■ Moses composed this blessing in gratitude for the manna with which God sustained the Jews in the wilderness. It was adopted as the first of the four blessings which make up Bircas HaMazon recited after all meals.

BORUCH ato Adōnoy   בָּרוּךְ אַתָּה יהוה

Blessed are You, HASHEM,

Elōhaynu melech ho-ōlom,   אֱלֹהֵינוּ מֶלֶךְ הָעוֹלָם,

our God, King of the universe,

hazon es ho-ōlom kulō, b'tuvō,   הַזָּן אֶת הָעוֹלָם כֻּלּוֹ, בְּטוּבוֹ,

Who nourishes the entire world, in His goodness —

b'chayn b'chesed uvrachamim   בְּחֵן בְּחֶסֶד וּבְרַחֲמִים,

with grace, with kindness and with mercy.

hu nōsayn lechem l'chol bosor,   הוּא נֹתֵן לֶחֶם לְכָל בָּשָׂר,

He gives nourishment to all flesh,

ki l'ōlom chasdō.   כִּי לְעוֹלָם חַסְדּוֹ.

for His kindness is eternal.

Uvtuvō hagodōl,   וּבְטוּבוֹ הַגָּדוֹל,

And through His great goodness,

tomid lō chosar lonu,   תָּמִיד לֹא חָסַר לָנוּ,

we have never lacked,

v'al yechsar lonu   וְאַל יֶחְסַר לָנוּ

and may we never lack,

mozōn l'ōlom vo-ed.   מָזוֹן לְעוֹלָם וָעֶד.

nourishment, for all eternity.

ba-avur sh'mō hagodōl,   בַּעֲבוּר שְׁמוֹ הַגָּדוֹל,

For the sake of His Great Name,

ki hu Ayl zon umfarnays lakōl,   כִּי הוּא אֵל זָן וּמְפַרְנֵס לַכֹּל,

because He is God Who nourishes and sustains all,

u-maytiv lakōl,   וּמֵטִיב לַכֹּל,

and benefits all,

u-maychin mozōn   וּמֵכִין מָזוֹן

and He prepares food

l'chōl b'riyōsov asher boro.   לְכָל בְּרִיּוֹתָיו אֲשֶׁר בָּרָא.

for all of His creatures which He has created.

Boruch ato Adōnoy,

בָּרוּךְ אַתָּה יהוה,

Blessed are You, HASHEM,

hazon es hakōl.

הַזָּן אֶת הַכֹּל.

Who nourishes all.

ALL PRESENT RESPOND: Omayn — אָמֵן

■ "We Thank You" was written by Joshua when he led the nation across the Jordan into the "desirable, good and spacious land," "flowing with milk and honey."

NŌ-DE l'cho, Adōnoy Elōhaynu,

נוֹדֶה לְךָ, יהוה אֱלֹהֵינוּ,

We thank You, HASHEM, our God,

al shehinchalto la-avōsaynu

עַל שֶׁהִנְחַלְתָּ לַאֲבוֹתֵינוּ

because You have given to our forefathers as a heritage

eretz chemdo tōvo urchovo,

אֶרֶץ חֶמְדָּה טוֹבָה וּרְחָבָה,

a desirable, good and spacious Land;

V'al shehōtzaysonu

וְעַל שֶׁהוֹצֵאתָנוּ

because You removed us,

Adōnoy Elōhaynu

יהוה אֱלֹהֵינוּ

HASHEM, our God,

may-eretz mitzra-yim,

מֵאֶרֶץ מִצְרַיִם,

from the land of Egypt

ufdisonu mibays avodim,

וּפְדִיתָנוּ מִבֵּית עֲבָדִים,

and You redeemed us from the house of bondage;

v'al b'ris'cho

וְעַל בְּרִיתְךָ

and for Your covenant

shechosamto bivsoraynu,

שֶׁחָתַמְתָּ בִּבְשָׂרֵנוּ,

which You sealed in our flesh;

v'al tōros'cho shelimad-tonu,

וְעַל תּוֹרָתְךָ שֶׁלִּמַּדְתָּנוּ,

for Your Torah which You taught us

v'al chu-kecho shehōdatonu,

וְעַל חֻקֶּיךָ שֶׁהוֹדַעְתָּנוּ,

and for Your statutes which You made known to us;

v'al cha-yim chayn vo-chesed
shechōnantonu,

וְעַל חַיִּים חֵן וָחֶסֶד
שֶׁחוֹנַנְתָּנוּ,

for life, grace, and lovingkindness which You granted us;

v'al achilas mozōn

וְעַל אֲכִילַת מָזוֹן

and for the provision of food

צָפוּן בָּרֵךְ הַלֵּל נִרְצָה שֻׁלְחָן עוֹרֵךְ מַצָּה

ꜩatzo   mōtzi   roch'tzo   magid   yachatz   karpas   ur'chatz   kadaysh

sho-ato zon umfarnays
   ōsonu tomid,

שָׁאַתָּה זָן וּמְפַרְנֵס
אוֹתָנוּ תָּמִיד,

with which You nourish and sustain us constantly,

b'chol yōm uvchol ays
   uvchol sho-o.

בְּכָל יוֹם וּבְכָל עֵת
וּבְכָל שָׁעָה.

in every day, in every season, and in every hour.

V'AL HAKŌL, Adōnoy Elōhaynu, וְעַל הַכֹּל יהוה אֱלֹהֵינוּ

For all, HASHEM, our God,

anachnu mōdim loch,
   umvor'chim ōsoch,

אֲנַחְנוּ מוֹדִים לָךְ,
וּמְבָרְכִים אוֹתָךְ,

we thank You and bless You.

yisborach shimcho b'fi kol chai

יִתְבָּרַךְ שִׁמְךָ בְּפִי כָל חַי

May Your Name be blessed by the mouth of all the living,

tomid l'ōlom vo-ed.

תָּמִיד לְעוֹלָם וָעֶד.

continuously for all eternity.

Kakosuv: V'ochalto v'sovoto,

כַּכָּתוּב: וְאָכַלְתָּ וְשָׂבָעְתָּ,

As it is written: "And you shall eat and you shall be satisfied

u-vayrachto es Adōnoy Elōhecho,

וּבֵרַכְתָּ אֶת יהוה אֱלֹהֶיךָ,

and you shall bless HASHEM, your God,

al ho-oretz hatōvo asher
   nosan loch.

עַל הָאָרֶץ הַטֹּבָה אֲשֶׁר
נָתַן לָךְ.

for the good land which He gave you."

Boruch ato Adōnoy,

בָּרוּךְ אַתָּה יהוה,

Blessed are You, HASHEM,

al ho-oretz v'al hamozōn.

עַל הָאָרֶץ וְעַל הַמָּזוֹן.

for the land and for the nourishment.

ALL PRESENT RESPOND: Omayn — אָמֵן

■ "Have Mercy" was composed by King David who referred to "Your people Israel
... Your city Jerusalem ..." Upon completing construction of the Temple, King
Solomon added "the great and holy House upon which Your Name is called."

RACHAYM Adōnoy Elōhaynu
       רַחֵם יהוה אֱלֹהֵינוּ

Have mercy, HASHEM, our God,

nirtzo   halayl   **BORaych**   tzofun   shulchon ōraych   kōraych   morc

al yisro-ayl amecho,

עַל יִשְׂרָאֵל עַמֶּךָ,

on Israel Your people;

v'al y'rushola-yim i-recho,

וְעַל יְרוּשָׁלַיִם עִירֶךָ,

on Jerusalem, Your city;

v'al tziyōn mishkan k'vōdecho,

וְעַל צִיּוֹן מִשְׁכַּן כְּבוֹדֶךָ,

on Zion, the resting place of Your Glory;

v'al malchus bays dovid
m'shichecho,

וְעַל מַלְכוּת בֵּית דָּוִד
מְשִׁיחֶךָ,

on the monarchy of the house of David, Your anointed;

v'al haba-yis hagodōl v'hakodōsh

וְעַל הַבַּיִת הַגָּדוֹל וְהַקָּדוֹשׁ

and on the great and holy House

shenikro shimcho olov.

שֶׁנִּקְרָא שִׁמְךָ עָלָיו.

upon which Your Name is called.

Elōhaynu ovinu,

אֱלֹהֵינוּ אָבִינוּ

Our God, our Father —

r'aynu, zunaynu, parn'saynu

רְעֵנוּ זוּנֵנוּ פַּרְנְסֵנוּ

tend us, nourish us, sustain us,

v'chalk'laynu v'harvichaynu,

וְכַלְכְּלֵנוּ וְהַרְוִיחֵנוּ,

support us, relieve us;

v'harvach lonu Adōnoy Elōhaynu
m'hayro mikol tzorōsaynu.

וְהַרְוַח לָנוּ יהוה אֱלֹהֵינוּ
מְהֵרָה מִכָּל צָרוֹתֵינוּ.

grant us, HASHEM, our God, speedy relief from all our troubles.

V'no al tatzrichaynu,

וְנָא אַל תַּצְרִיכֵנוּ,

Please, make us not needful —

Adōnoy Elōhaynu,

יהוה אֱלֹהֵינוּ,

HASHEM, our God —

lō liday mat'nas bosor vodom,

לֹא לִידֵי מַתְּנַת בָּשָׂר וָדָם,

of the gifts of human hands

v'lō liday halvo-osom,

וְלֹא לִידֵי הַלְוָאָתָם,

nor of their loans,

ki im l'yod'cho

כִּי אִם לְיָדְךָ

but only of Your Hand

ham'lay-o hap'su-cho

הַמְּלֵאָה הַפְּתוּחָה

that is full, open,

hak'dōsho v'hor'chovo,　　　　　　　הַקְּדוֹשָׁה וְהָרְחָבָה,
holy and generous,

shelō nayvōsh v'lō nikolaym　　　　שֶׁלֹּא נֵבוֹשׁ וְלֹא נִכָּלֵם
that we not feel inner shame nor be humiliated

l'ōlom vo-ed.　　　　　　　　　　　לְעוֹלָם וָעֶד.
forever and ever.

ON THE SABBATH ADD THE FOLLOWING PARAGRAPH.

R'TZAY v'hachalitzaynu　　　　　רְצֵה וְהַחֲלִיצֵנוּ
Adōnoy Elōhaynu　　　　　　　　　　יהוה אֱלֹהֵינוּ
May it please You, HASHEM, our God — give us rest

b'mitzvōsecho,　　　　　　　　　　　בְּמִצְוֹתֶיךָ,
through Your commandments

uvmitzvas yōm hash'vi-i　　　　　　וּבְמִצְוַת יוֹם הַשְּׁבִיעִי
and through the commandment of the seventh day,

ha-shabos hagodōl　　　　　　　　　הַשַּׁבָּת הַגָּדוֹל
v'hakodōsh ha-ze,　　　　　　　　　וְהַקָּדוֹשׁ הַזֶּה,
this great and holy Sabbath.

ki yōm ze　　　　　　　　　　　　　כִּי יוֹם זֶה
For this day

godōl v'kodōsh hu l'fonecho,　　　גָּדוֹל וְקָדוֹשׁ הוּא לְפָנֶיךָ,
is great and holy before You

lishbos bō v'lonu-ach　　　　　　　לִשְׁבָּת בּוֹ וְלָנוּחַ
bō b'ahavo　　　　　　　　　　　　בּוֹ בְּאַהֲבָה
to rest on it and be content on it in love,

k'mitzvas r'tzōnecho.　　　　　　　כְּמִצְוַת רְצוֹנֶךָ.
as ordained by Your will.

U-virtzōn'cho honi-ach lonu,　　　וּבִרְצוֹנְךָ הָנִיחַ לָנוּ,
May this be Your will — calm us,

Adōnoy Elōhaynu,　　　　　　　　　יהוה אֱלֹהֵינוּ,
HASHEM, our God,

shelō s'hay tzoro v'yogōn　　　　שֶׁלֹּא תְהֵא צָרָה וְיָגוֹן
va-anocho　　　　　　　　　　　　וַאֲנָחָה
so that there be no distress, grief, or lament

יחר כּורךְ שֻׁלְחָן עוֹרֵךְ צָפוּן בַּרֵךְ הַלֵּל נִרְצָה
nirtzo　halayl　BORAYCH　tzofun　shulchon ōraych　kōraych　morō

b'yōm m'nuchosaynu.

בְּיוֹם מְנוּחָתֵנוּ.

on this day of our contentment.

V'har-aynu Adōnoy Elōhaynu

וְהַרְאֵנוּ יהוה אֱלֹהֵינוּ

And show us, HASHEM, our God,

b'nechomas tziyōn i-recho,

בְּנֶחָמַת צִיּוֹן עִירֶךָ,

the consolation of Zion, Your city,

uv'vinyan y'rushola-yim

וּבְבִנְיַן יְרוּשָׁלַיִם

and the rebuilding of Jerusalem,

ir kodshecho,

עִיר קָדְשֶׁךָ,

City of Your holiness,

ki ato hu ba-al hai-shu-ōs

כִּי אַתָּה הוּא בַּעַל הַיְשׁוּעוֹת

for You are the Master of salvations

uva-al hanechomōs.

וּבַעַל הַנֶּחָמוֹת.

and Master of consolations.

■ May our lot rise above the ordinary; come before God, reach Him and be noted by Him in the best of lights, worthy of his favor. May He hear the impact on our lives, consider our needs and remember our relationship to Him.

ELŌHAYNU Vaylōhay avōsaynu, אֱלֹהֵינוּ וֵאלֹהֵי אֲבוֹתֵינוּ,

Our God and the God of our forefathers,

ya-a-le v'yovō v'yagi-a v'yayro-e יַעֲלֶה, וְיָבֹא, וְיַגִּיעַ, וְיֵרָאֶה,

may there rise, come, reach, be noted,

v'yayro-tze v'yi-shoma v'yipokayd וְיֵרָצֶה, וְיִשָּׁמַע, וְיִפָּקֵד,

be favored, be heard, be considered

v'yizochayr zichrōnaynu u-fikdōnaynu, וְיִזָּכֵר זִכְרוֹנֵנוּ וּפִקְדוֹנֵנוּ,

and be remembered — the remembrance and consideration of ourselves;

v'zichrōn avōsaynu, וְזִכְרוֹן אֲבוֹתֵינוּ,

the remembrance of our forefathers;

v'zichrōn moshi-ach וְזִכְרוֹן מָשִׁיחַ

ben dovid avdecho, בֶּן דָּוִד עַבְדֶּךָ,

the remembrance of Messiah, son of David, Your servant;

v'zichrōn y'rushola-yim וְזִכְרוֹן יְרוּשָׁלַיִם

ir kod-shecho, עִיר קָדְשֶׁךָ,

the remembrance of Jerusalem, Your Holy City;

קַדֵּשׁ וּרְחַץ כַּרְפַּס יַחַץ מַגִּיד רָחְצָה מוֹצִיא מַצ

atzo mōtzi roch'tzo magid yachatz karpas ur'chatz kadaysh

v'zichrōn kol am'cho
   bays yisro-ayl l'fonecho,
      and the remembrance of Your entire people the Family of Israel — before You
וְזִכְרוֹן כָּל עַמְּךָ
בֵּית יִשְׂרָאֵל לְפָנֶיךָ,

lif-layto l'tōvo
      for deliverance, for goodness,
לִפְלֵיטָה לְטוֹבָה

l'chayn ulchesed ulrachamim,
      for grace, for kindness, and for compassion,
לְחֵן וּלְחֶסֶד וּלְרַחֲמִים,

l'cha-yim ulsholōm
      for life, and for peace
לְחַיִּים וּלְשָׁלוֹם

b'yōm chag hamatzōs ha-ze.
      on this day of the Festival of Matzos.
בְּיוֹם חַג הַמַּצּוֹת הַזֶּה.

zoch'raynu Adōnoy Elōhaynu
   bō l'tōvo,
      Remember us on it, HASHEM, our God, for goodness,
זָכְרֵנוּ יהוה אֱלֹהֵינוּ
בּוֹ לְטוֹבָה,

u-fokdaynu vō livrocho,
      consider us on it for blessing
וּפָקְדֵנוּ בּוֹ לִבְרָכָה,

v'hōshi-aynu vō l'cha-yim.
      and help us on it for life.
וְהוֹשִׁיעֵנוּ בּוֹ לְחַיִּים.

U-vidvar y'shu-o v'rachamim,
      In the matter of salvation and compassion,
וּבִדְבַר יְשׁוּעָה וְרַחֲמִים,

chus v'chonaynu v'rachaym olaynu
   v'hōshi-aynu,
      pity, be gracious and compassionate with us and help us,
חוּס וְחָנֵּנוּ וְרַחֵם עָלֵינוּ
וְהוֹשִׁיעֵנוּ,

ki aylecho aynaynu,
      for our eyes are turned to You,
כִּי אֵלֶיךָ עֵינֵינוּ,

ki Ayl chanun
   v'rachum oto.
      because You are God, the gracious and compassionate.
כִּי אֵל חַנּוּן
וְרַחוּם אָתָּה.

UVNAY y'rushola-yim ir hakōdesh
      Rebuild Jerusalem, the Holy City,
וּבְנֵה יְרוּשָׁלַיִם עִיר הַקֹּדֶשׁ

bimhayro v'yomaynu.
      soon in our days.
בִּמְהֵרָה בְיָמֵינוּ.

nirtzo   halayl   **BORaych**   tzofun   shulchon ōraych   kōraych   morōr

Boruch ato Adōnoy, בָּרוּךְ אַתָּה יהוה,

Blessed are You, HASHEM,

bōnay (v'rachamov) y'rusholo-yim. בּוֹנֵה (בְּרַחֲמָיו) יְרוּשָׁלָיִם.

Who rebuilds Jerusalem (in His mercy).

Omayn. אָמֵן.

Amen.

ALL PRESENT RESPOND: Omayn — אָמֵן

■ It is insufficient to thank God for His graciousness and beneficence to past generations. We must be aware that His goodness and bounty are daily, constant occurrences — and will always be so.

BORUCH ato Adōnoy בָּרוּךְ אַתָּה יהוה

Blessed are You, HASHEM,

Elōhaynu melech ho-ōlom, אֱלֹהֵינוּ מֶלֶךְ הָעוֹלָם,

our God, King of the universe,

ho-Ayl ovinu malkaynu הָאֵל אָבִינוּ מַלְכֵּנוּ

the Almighty, our Father, our King,

adiraynu bōr'aynu אַדִירֵנוּ בּוֹרְאֵנוּ

our Sovereign, our Creator,

gō-alaynu yōtz'raynu, גּוֹאֲלֵנוּ יוֹצְרֵנוּ,

our Redeemer, our Maker,

k'dōshaynu k'dōsh ya-akōv, קְדוֹשֵׁנוּ קְדוֹשׁ יַעֲקֹב,

our Holy One, Holy One of Jacob,

rō-aynu rō-ay yisro-ayl. רוֹעֵנוּ רוֹעֵה יִשְׂרָאֵל.

our Shepherd, the Shepherd of Israel.

Hamelech hatōv הַמֶּלֶךְ הַטּוֹב

The King Who is good

v'hamaytiv lakōl, וְהַמֵּטִיב לַכֹּל,

and Who does good for all,

sheb'chol yōm vo-yōm שֶׁבְּכָל יוֹם וָיוֹם

for every single day

hu haytiv, hu maytiv, הוּא הֵטִיב, הוּא מֵטִיב,

He did good, He does good,

hu yaytiv lonu. הוּא יֵיטִיב לָנוּ.

and He will do good to us.

קַדֵּשׁ וּרְחַץ כַּרְפַּס יַחַץ מַגִּיד רָחְצָה מוֹצִיא מַצָּה

atzo mōtzi roch'tzo magid yachatz karpas ur'chatz kadaysh

Hu g'molonu, hu gōm'laynu,   הוּא גְמָלָנוּ, הוּא גוֹמְלֵנוּ,

He was bountiful with us, He is bountiful with us,

hu yigm'laynu lo-ad,   הוּא יִגְמְלֵנוּ לָעַד,

and He will forever be bountiful with us —

l'chayn ulchesed   לְחֵן וּלְחֶסֶד

with grace and with kindness,

ulrachamim ulrevach,   וּלְרַחֲמִים וּלְרֶוַח,

with mercy and with relief,

hatzolo v'hatzlocho,   הַצָּלָה וְהַצְלָחָה,

salvation, success,

b'rocho vi-shu-o,   בְּרָכָה וִישׁוּעָה

blessing, help,

nechomo, parnoso v'chalkolo,   נֶחָמָה פַּרְנָסָה וְכַלְכָּלָה

consolation, sustenance, support,

v'rachamim v'cha-yim   וְרַחֲמִים וְחַיִּים

mercy, life,

v'sholōm v'chol tōv,   וְשָׁלוֹם וְכָל טוֹב,

peace and all good;

u-mikol tuv   וּמִכָּל טוֹב

and of all good things

l'ōlom al y'chas'raynu.   לְעוֹלָם אַל יְחַסְּרֵנוּ.

may He never deprive us.

ALL PRESENT RESPOND: Omayn — אָמֵן

HORACHAMON,   הָרַחֲמָן,

The compassionate One!

hu yimlōch olaynu   הוּא יִמְלוֹךְ עָלֵינוּ
l'ōlom vo-ed.   לְעוֹלָם וָעֶד.

May He reign over us forever.

Horachamon, hu yisborach   הָרַחֲמָן, הוּא יִתְבָּרַךְ

The compassionate One! May He be blessed

bashoma-yim uvo-oretz.   בַּשָּׁמַיִם וּבָאָרֶץ.

in heaven and on earth.

Horachamon,   הָרַחֲמָן,

The compassionate One!

nirtzo   halayl   **BORAych**   tzofun   shulchon ōraych   kōraych   mor

hu yishtabach l'dōr dōrim,
הוּא יִשְׁתַּבַּח לְדוֹר דּוֹרִים,
May He be praised throughout all generations,

v'yispo-ar bonu lo-ad
וְיִתְפָּאַר בָּנוּ לָעַד
and may He be glorified through us forever

ulnaytzach n'tzochim,
וּלְנֵצַח נְצָחִים,
to the ultimate ends,

v'yis-hadar bonu lo-ad
וְיִתְהַדַּר בָּנוּ לָעַד
and be honored through us forever

ul-ōl'may ōlomim.
וּלְעוֹלְמֵי עוֹלָמִים.
and for all eternity.

Horachamon,
הָרַחֲמָן
The compassionate One!

hu y'farn'saynu b'chovōd.
הוּא יְפַרְנְסֵנוּ בְּכָבוֹד.
May He sustain us in honor.

Horachamon,
הָרַחֲמָן,
The compassionate One!

hu yishbōr ulaynu
הוּא יִשְׁבּוֹר עָלֵינוּ
may-al tzavoraynu,
מֵעַל צַוָּארֵנוּ,
May He break the yoke of oppression from our necks

v'hu yōli-chaynu
וְהוּא יוֹלִיכֵנוּ
kōm'miyus l'artzaynu.
קוֹמְמִיּוּת לְאַרְצֵנוּ.
and guide us erect to our Land.

Horachamon,
הָרַחֲמָן,
The compassionate One!

hu yishlach lonu b'rocho
הוּא יִשְׁלַח לָנוּ בְּרָכָה
m'rubo baba-yis ha-ze,
מְרֻבָּה בַּבַּיִת הַזֶּה,
May He send us abundant blessing to this house

v'al shulchon ze she-ochalnu olov.
וְעַל שֻׁלְחָן זֶה שֶׁאָכַלְנוּ עָלָיו.
and upon this table at which we have eaten.

Horachamon,
הָרַחֲמָן,
The compassionate One!

hu yishlach lonu es
הוּא יִשְׁלַח לָנוּ אֶת
ayliyohu hanovi zochur latōv,
אֵלִיָּהוּ הַנָּבִיא זָכוּר לַטּוֹב,
May He send us Elijah, the Prophet — he is remembered for good —

קַדֵּשׁ וּרְחַץ כַּרְפַּס יַחַץ מַגִּיד רָחְצָה מוֹצִיא מַצָּ
tzo mōtzi roch'tzo magid yachatz karpas ur'chatz kadaysh

vivaser lonu b'sōrōs tōvōs וִיבַשֵּׂר לָנוּ בְּשׂוֹרוֹת טוֹבוֹת

to proclaim to us good tidings,

y'shu-ōs v'nechomōs. יְשׁוּעוֹת וְנֶחָמוֹת.

salvations, and consolations.

AT ONE'S OWN TABLE (INCLUDE THE APPLICABLE WORDS IN PARENTHESES):

Horachamon, הָרַחֲמָן,

The compassionate One!

hu y'voraych ōsi הוּא יְבָרֵךְ אוֹתִי

May He bless me

(v'es ishti/v'es bali v'es zari) (וְאֶת אִשְׁתִּי/וְאֶת בַּעְלִי וְאֶת זַרְעִי)

(my wife/husband and my children)

v'es kol asher li. וְאֶת כָּל אֲשֶׁר לִי.

and all that is mine.

■ The Patriarchs were blessed in every possible way. "And Hashem blessed Abraham in everything." Isaac declared, "I have partaken from everything." And Jacob said, "God has been gracious to me and I have everything." So may we be blessed.

GUESTS RECITE THE FOLLOWING (CHILDREN AT THEIR PARENTS' TABLE INCLUDE THE APPLICABLE WORDS IN PARENTHESES):

Horachamon, הָרַחֲמָן,

The compassionate One!

hu y'voraych es (ovi mōri) הוּא יְבָרֵךְ אֶת (אָבִי מוֹרִי)
  ba-al haba-yis ha-ze, בַּעַל הַבַּיִת הַזֶּה,

May He bless (my father, my teacher) the master of this house,

v'es (imi mōrosi) וְאֶת (אִמִּי מוֹרָתִי)
  ba-alas haba-yis ha-ze, בַּעֲלַת הַבַּיִת הַזֶּה,

and (my mother, my teacher) lady of this house,

ALL CONTINUE:

ōsom v'es baysom v'es zar-om אוֹתָם וְאֶת בֵּיתָם וְאֶת זַרְעָם

them, their house, their family

v'es kol asher lohem, וְאֶת כָּל אֲשֶׁר לָהֶם,

and all that is theirs,

ōsonu v'es kol asher lonu, אוֹתָנוּ וְאֶת כָּל אֲשֶׁר לָנוּ,

ours and all that is ours —

nirtzo   halayl   **BORaych**   tzofun   shulchon ōraych   kōraych   morō

k'mō shenisbor'chu avōsaynu
כְּמוֹ שֶׁנִּתְבָּרְכוּ אֲבוֹתֵינוּ

avrohom yitzchok v'ya-akōv
אַבְרָהָם יִצְחָק וְיַעֲקֹב

just as our forefathers Abraham, Isaac and Jacob were blessed

bakōl mikōl kōl.
בַּכֹּל מִכֹּל כֹּל,

in everything, from everything, with everything.

kayn y'voraych ōsonu kulonu yachad
כֵּן יְבָרֵךְ אוֹתָנוּ כֻּלָּנוּ יַחַד

So may He bless us all together

bivrocho sh'laymo.
בִּבְרָכָה שְׁלֵמָה.

with a perfect blessing.

V'nōmar: Omayn.
וְנֹאמַר: אָמֵן.

And let us say: Amen!

BAMORŌM
בַּמָּרוֹם

On high,

y'lam'du alayhem v'olaynu z'chus,
יְלַמְּדוּ עֲלֵיהֶם וְעָלֵינוּ זְכוּת,

may merit be pleaded upon them and upon us,

shet'hay l'mishmeres sholōm,
שֶׁתְּהֵא לְמִשְׁמֶרֶת שָׁלוֹם,

for a safeguard of peace.

V'niso v'rocho may-ays Adōnoy,
וְנִשָּׂא בְרָכָה מֵאֵת יהוה,

May we receive a blessing from HASHEM

utzdoko may-Elōhay yish-aynu,
וּצְדָקָה מֵאֱלֹהֵי יִשְׁעֵנוּ,

and just kindness from the God of our salvation,

v'nimtzo chayn v'saychel tōv
וְנִמְצָא חֵן וְשֵׂכֶל טוֹב

and find favor and good understanding

b'aynay Elōhim v'odom.
בְּעֵינֵי אֱלֹהִים וְאָדָם.

in the eyes of God and man.

ON THE SABBATH ADD:

Horachamon, hu yanchilaynu
הָרַחֲמָן, הוּא יַנְחִילֵנוּ

The compassionate One! May He cause us to inherit

yōm shekulō shabos umnucho
יוֹם שֶׁכֻּלוֹ שַׁבָּת וּמְנוּחָה

the day which will be completely a Sabbath and rest day

l'cha-yay ho-ōlomim.
לְחַיֵּי הָעוֹלָמִים.

for eternal life.

קַדֵּשׁ וּרְחַץ כַּרְפַּס יַחַץ מַגִּיד רָחְצָה מוֹצִיא מַצָ

atzo   mōtzi   roch'tzo   magid   yachatz   karpas   ur'chatz   kadaysh

HORACHAMON, hu yanchilaynu   הָרַחֲמָן הוּא יַנְחִילֵנוּ

The compassionate One! May He cause us to inherit

yōm shekulō tōv.   יוֹם שֶׁכֻּלּוֹ טוֹב.

the day which is completely good.

HORACHAMON, hu y'zakaynu   הָרַחֲמָן הוּא יְזַכֵּנוּ

The compassionate One! May He make us worthy

limōs hamoshi-ach   לִימוֹת הַמָּשִׁיחַ

of the days of Messiah

ulcha-yay ho-ōlom habo.   וּלְחַיֵּי הָעוֹלָם הַבָּא.

and the life of the World to Come.

Migdōl y'shu-ōs malkō,   מִגְדּוֹל יְשׁוּעוֹת מַלְכּוֹ

He Who is a tower of salvations to His king

v'ōse chesed limshichō   וְעֹשֶׂה חֶסֶד לִמְשִׁיחוֹ

and does kindness for His anointed,

l'dovid ulzar-ō ad ōlom.   לְדָוִד וּלְזַרְעוֹ עַד עוֹלָם.

to David and to his descendants forever.

Ō-se sholōm bimrōmov,   עֹשֶׂה שָׁלוֹם בִּמְרוֹמָיו,

He Who makes peace in His heights,

hu ya-a-se sholōm olaynu   הוּא יַעֲשֶׂה שָׁלוֹם עָלֵינוּ

may He make peace upon us

v'al kol yisro-ayl.   וְעַל כָּל יִשְׂרָאֵל.

and upon all Israel.

V'imru: Omayn.   וְאִמְרוּ, אָמֵן.

Now respond: Amen!

Y'RU es Adōnoy k'dōshov,   יְראוּ אֶת יהוה קְדֹשָׁיו,

Fear HASHEM, you — His holy ones —

ki ayn machsōr liray-ov.   כִּי אֵין מַחְסוֹר לִירֵאָיו.

for there is no deprivation for His reverent ones.

K'firim roshu v'ro-ayvu,   כְּפִירִים רָשׁוּ וְרָעֵבוּ,

Young lions may be in need and hunger,

v'dōr'shay Adōnoy   וְדֹרְשֵׁי יהוה

but those who seek HASHEM

nirtzo   haLayL   BORaych   tzofun   shuLchon ōraych   kōraych   moror lō yachs'ru chol tōv.

לֹא יַחְסְרוּ כָל טוֹב.

will not lack any good.

Hōdu La-dōnoy ki tōv,

הוֹדוּ לַיהוה כִּי טוֹב,

Give thanks to God for He is good;

ki l'ōlom chasdō.

כִּי לְעוֹלָם חַסְדּוֹ.

His kindness endures forever.

Pōsay-ach es yodecho,

פּוֹתֵחַ אֶת יָדֶךָ,

You open Your hand

u-masbi-a l'chol chai rotzōn.

וּמַשְׂבִּיעַ לְכָל חַי רָצוֹן.

and satisfy the desire of every living thing.

Boruch hagever
asher yivtach Ba-dōnoy,

בָּרוּךְ הַגֶּבֶר
אֲשֶׁר יִבְטַח בַּיהוה,

Blessed is the man who trusts in HASHEM,

v'ho-yo Adōnoy mivtachō.

וְהָיָה יהוה מִבְטַחוֹ.

then HASHEM will be his security.

Na-ar ho-yisi gam zokanti,

נַעַר הָיִיתִי גַּם זָקַנְתִּי,

I was a youth and also have aged,

v'lō ro-isi tzadik ne-ezov,

וְלֹא רָאִיתִי צַדִּיק נֶעֱזָב,

and I have not seen a righteous man forsaken,

v'zar-ō m'vakaysh lochem.

וְזַרְעוֹ מְבַקֶּשׁ לָחֶם.

with his children begging for bread.

Adōnoy ōz l'amō yitayn,

יהוה עֹז לְעַמּוֹ יִתֵּן,

HASHEM will give might to His people;

Adōnoy y'voraych es amō
va-sholōm.

יהוה יְבָרֵךְ אֶת עַמּוֹ
בַשָּׁלוֹם.

HASHEM will bless His people with peace.

UPON COMPLETION OF BIRCAS HAMAZON THE BLESSING OVER WINE IS RECITED AND THE
THIRD CUP IS DRUNK WHILE RECLINING ON THE LEFT SIDE. IT IS PREFERABLE TO DRINK THE
ENTIRE CUP, BUT AT THE VERY LEAST, MOST OF THE CUP SHOULD BE DRAINED.

BORUCH ato Adōnoy

בָּרוּךְ אַתָּה יהוה

Blessed are You, HASHEM

Elōhaynu melech ho-ōlom

אֱלֹהֵינוּ מֶלֶךְ הָעוֹלָם,

our God, King of the universe,

bōray p'riy hagofen.

בּוֹרֵא פְּרִי הַגָּפֶן.

Who creates the the fruit of the vine.

קַדֵּשׁ וּרְחַץ כַּרְפַּס יַחַץ מַגִּיד רָחְצָה מוֹצִיא מַצָּ

atzo mōtzi roch'tzo magid yachatz karpas ur'chatz kadaysh

THE FOURTH CUP IS POURED. ACCORDING TO MOST CUSTOMS, THE CUP OF ELIJAH IS POURED AT THIS POINT, AFTER WHICH THE DOOR IS OPENED IN ACCORDANCE WITH THE VERSE *"IT IS A GUARDED NIGHT,"* AND THE FOLLOWING PARAGRAPH IS RECITED.

■ Past redemption from Egypt was the theme of the part of the Haggadah recited before the meal. Now, the tense switches and the future Messianic redemption is brought to the fore. We open the door, indicating our readiness to receive the Prophet Elijah, herald of the Messiah, as we beseech God to pour His wrath upon those who would play Pharaoh's spiritual successors in oppressing the Jews.

SH'FŌCH chamos'cho   שְׁפֹךְ חֲמָתְךָ
Pour forth Your wrath

el hagō-yim asher lō y'do-ucho   אֶל הַגּוֹיִם אֲשֶׁר לֹא יְדָעוּךָ
upon the nations that do not recognize You,

v'al mamlochōs   וְעַל מַמְלָכוֹת
and upon the kingdoms

asher b'shimcho lō koro-u.   אֲשֶׁר בְּשִׁמְךָ לֹא קָרָאוּ.
that do not invoke Your name.

Ki ochal es ya-akōv   כִּי אָכַל אֶת יַעֲקֹב
For they have devoured Jacob

v'es novayhu hayshamu.   וְאֶת נָוֵהוּ הֵשַׁמּוּ.
and destroyed His Habitation.

Sh'foch alayhem za-mecho   שְׁפָךְ עֲלֵיהֶם זַעְמֶךָ
Pour forth Your indignation upon them

vacharōn ap'cho yasigaym.   וַחֲרוֹן אַפְּךָ יַשִּׂיגֵם.
and let Your burning wrath overtake them.

Tirdōf b'af v'sashmidaym   תִּרְדֹּף בְּאַף וְתַשְׁמִידֵם
Pursue them with anger and destroy them

mitachas sh'may Adōnoy.   מִתַּחַת שְׁמֵי יהוה.
from beneath the heavens of HASHEM.

هلل / **HALAYL**

THE DOOR IS CLOSED AND THE RECITATION OF THE HAGGADAH IS CONTINUED.

■ The ideas and ideals which distinguish us from the other nations are highlighted as we plead for the future redemption — not for our sake, but to sanctify God's Name.

LŌ LONU, Adōnoy, lō lonu,   לֹא לָנוּ, יהוה, לֹא לָנוּ,
Not for our sake, HASHEM, not for our sake,

nirtzo   halayl   Boraych   tzofun   shulchon ōraych   kōraych   mor

ki l'shimcho tayn kovōd,
כִּי לְשִׁמְךָ תֵּן כָּבוֹד,

but for Your Name's sake give glory,

al chasd'cho al amitecho.
עַל חַסְדְּךָ עַל אֲמִתֶּךָ.

for Your kindness and for Your truth!

Lomo yōm'ru hagōyim,
לָמָּה יֹאמְרוּ הַגּוֹיִם,

Why should the nations say,

a-yay no Elōhayhem.
אַיֵּה נָא אֱלֹהֵיהֶם.

"Where is their God now?"

Vaylōhaynu va-shomo-yim,
וֵאלֹהֵינוּ בַשָּׁמָיִם,

Our God is in the heavens;

kōl asher chofaytz oso.
כֹּל אֲשֶׁר חָפֵץ עָשָׂה.

whatever He pleases, He does!

Atzabayhem kesef v'zohov,
עֲצַבֵּיהֶם כֶּסֶף וְזָהָב,

ma-asay y'day odom.
מַעֲשֵׂה יְדֵי אָדָם.

Their idols are silver and gold, the handiwork of man.

Pe lohem v'lō y'dabayru,
פֶּה לָהֶם וְלֹא יְדַבֵּרוּ,

They have a mouth, but cannot speak;

ayna-yim lohem v'lō yir-u.
עֵינַיִם לָהֶם וְלֹא יִרְאוּ.

they have eyes, but cannot see.

Ozna-yim lohem v'lō yishmo-u,
אָזְנַיִם לָהֶם וְלֹא יִשְׁמָעוּ,

They have ears, but cannot hear;

af lohem v'lō y'ri-chun.
אַף לָהֶם וְלֹא יְרִיחוּן.

they have a nose, but cannot smell.

Y'dayhem v'lō y'mi-shun,
יְדֵיהֶם וְלֹא יְמִישׁוּן,

Their hands — they cannot feel;

raglayhem v'lō y'halaychu,
רַגְלֵיהֶם וְלֹא יְהַלֵּכוּ,

their feet — they cannot walk;

lō yehgu bigrōnom.
לֹא יֶהְגּוּ בִּגְרוֹנָם.

they cannot utter a sound from their throat.

K'mōhem yih-yu ōsayhem,
כְּמוֹהֶם יִהְיוּ עֹשֵׂיהֶם,

Those who make them should become like them,

kōl asher bōtay-ach bohem.
כֹּל אֲשֶׁר בֹּטֵחַ בָּהֶם.

whoever trusts in them!

קַדֵּשׁ וּרְחַץ כַּרְפַּס יַחַץ מַגִּיד רָחְצָה מוֹצִיא מַ

...tzo mōtzi roch'tzo magid yachatz karpas ur'chatz kadaysh

Yisro-ayl b'tach Ba-dōnoy, יִשְׂרָאֵל בְּטַח בַּיהוה,

O Israel, trust in HASHEM;

ezrom u-moginom hu. עֶזְרָם וּמָגִנָּם הוּא.

their help and their shield is He!

Bays aharōn bit-chu Va-dōnoy, בֵּית אַהֲרֹן בִּטְחוּ בַיהוה,

House of Aaron, trust in HASHEM;

ezrom u-moginom hu. עֶזְרָם וּמָגִנָּם הוּא.

their help and their shield is He!

Yir-ay Adōnoy bit-chu Va-dōnoy, יִרְאֵי יהוה בִּטְחוּ בַיהוה,

You who fear HASHEM, trust in HASHEM;

ezrom u-moginom hu. עֶזְרָם וּמָגִנָּם הוּא.

their help and their shield is He!

■ We are confident that Hashem blesses Israel, and pledge that as long as we have the gift of life, we will praise Him.

ADŌNOY z'choronu y'voraych, יהוה זְכָרָנוּ יְבָרֵךְ,

HASHEM Who has remembered us will bless —

y'voraych es bays yisro-ayl, יְבָרֵךְ אֶת בֵּית יִשְׂרָאֵל,

He will bless the House of Israel;

y'voraych es bays aharōn. יְבָרֵךְ אֶת בֵּית אַהֲרֹן.

He will bless the House of Aaron;

Y'voraych yir-ay Adōnoy, יְבָרֵךְ יִרְאֵי יהוה,

hak'tanim im hag'dōlim. הַקְּטַנִּים עִם הַגְּדֹלִים.

He will bless those who fear HASHEM, the small as well as the great.

Yōsayf Adōnoy alaychem, יֹסֵף יהוה עֲלֵיכֶם,

alaychem v'al b'naychem. עֲלֵיכֶם וְעַל בְּנֵיכֶם.

May HASHEM increase upon you, upon you and upon your children!

B'ruchim atem La-dōnoy, בְּרוּכִים אַתֶּם לַיהוה,

You are blessed of HASHEM,

ōsay shoma-yim vo-oretz. עֹשֵׂה שָׁמַיִם וָאָרֶץ.

maker of heaven and earth.

Ha-shoma-yim shoma-yim La-dōnoy, הַשָּׁמַיִם שָׁמַיִם לַיהוה,

As for the heavens — the heavens are HASHEM's,

nirtzo   halayl   BORaych   tzofun   shulchon ōraych   kōraych   moro

v'ho-oretz nosan livnay odom.

וְהָאָרֶץ נָתַן לִבְנֵי אָדָם.

but the earth He has given to mankind.

Lō ha-maysim y'hal'lu Yoh,

לֹא הַמֵּתִים יְהַלְלוּ יָהּ,

Neither the dead can praise God,

v'lō kol yōr'day dumo.

וְלֹא כָּל יֹרְדֵי דוּמָה.

nor any who descend into silence;

Va-anachnu n'voraych Yoh,

וַאֲנַחְנוּ נְבָרֵךְ יָהּ,

but we will bless God

may-ato v'ad ōlom,

מֵעַתָּה וְעַד עוֹלָם,

from this time and forever.

hal'luyoh.

הַלְלוּיָהּ.

Praise God!

■ The recollection of dangers past, overcome through the help of God, endows us with an unshakeable trust in His salvation from our present distress. As we approach the future we are secure in our faith.

OHAVTI ki yishma Adōnoy
es kōli tachanunoy.

אָהַבְתִּי כִּי יִשְׁמַע יהוה
אֶת קוֹלִי תַּחֲנוּנָי.

I love [Him], for HASHEM hears my voice, my supplications.

Ki hito oznō li, uvyomai ekro.

כִּי הִטָּה אָזְנוֹ לִי, וּבְיָמַי אֶקְרָא.

As He has inclined His ear to me, so in my days shall I call.

Afofuni chevlay mo-ves,

אֲפָפוּנִי חֶבְלֵי מָוֶת,

The pains of death encircled me;

umtzoray sh'ōl m'tzo-uni,

וּמְצָרֵי שְׁאוֹל מְצָאוּנִי,

the confines of the grave have found me;

tzoro v'yogōn emtzo.

צָרָה וְיָגוֹן אֶמְצָא.

trouble and sorrow I would find.

Uvshaym Adōnoy ekro,

וּבְשֵׁם יהוה אֶקְרָא,

Then I would invoke the Name of HASHEM:

ono Adōnoy mal'to nafshi.

אָנָּה יהוה מַלְּטָה נַפְשִׁי.

"Please, HASHEM, save my soul."

Chanun Adōnoy v'tzadik,
Vaylōhaynu m'rachaym.

חַנּוּן יהוה וְצַדִּיק,
וֵאלֹהֵינוּ מְרַחֵם.

Gracious is HASHEM and righteous, our God is merciful.

קַדֵּשׁ וּרְחַץ כַּרְפַּס יַחַץ מַגִּיד רָחְצָה מוֹצִיא מַצ
tzo   mōtzi   roch'tzo   magid   yachatz   karpas   ur'chatz   kadaysh

Shōmayr p'so-yim Adōnoy,

שֹׁמֵר פְּתָאיִם יהוה,

HASHEM protects the simple;

dalōsi v'li y'hōshi-a.

דַּלוֹתִי וְלִי יְהוֹשִׁיעַ.

I was brought low, but He saved me.

Shuvi nafshi limnuchoychi,

שׁוּבִי נַפְשִׁי לִמְנוּחָיְכִי,

Return, my soul, to your rest;

ki Adōnoy gomal oloychi.

כִּי יהוה גָּמַל עָלָיְכִי.

for HASHEM has been kind to you.

Ki chilatzto nafshi mimo-ves,

כִּי חִלַּצְתָּ נַפְשִׁי מִמָּוֶת,

For You have delivered my soul from death,

es ayni min dim-o,

אֶת עֵינִי מִן דִּמְעָה,

   es ragli midechi.

אֶת רַגְלִי מִדֶּחִי.

my eyes from tears, my feet from stumbling.

Es-halaych lifnay Adōnoy,

אֶתְהַלֵּךְ לִפְנֵי יהוה,

I shall walk before HASHEM

b'artzōs hacha-yim.

בְּאַרְצוֹת הַחַיִּים.

in the lands of the living.

He-emanti ki adabayr,

הֶאֱמַנְתִּי כִּי אֲדַבֵּר,

I have kept faith although I say:

ani onisi m'ōd.

אֲנִי עָנִיתִי מְאֹד.

"I suffer exceedingly."

Ani omarti v'chofzi,

אֲנִי אָמַרְתִּי בְחָפְזִי,

I said in my haste:

kol ho-odom kōzayv.

כָּל הָאָדָם כֹּזֵב.

"All mankind is deceitful."

■ How shall we express our thanks? By praising Him with words and deeds, and by praying for His Temple to be rebuilt that we may worship there.

MO OSHIV La-dōnoy,

מָה אָשִׁיב לַיהוה,

How can I repay HASHEM

kol tagmulōhi oloy.

כָּל תַּגְמוּלוֹהִי עָלָי.

for all His kindness to me?

Kōs y'shu-ōs eso,

כּוֹס יְשׁוּעוֹת אֶשָּׂא,

I will raise the cup of salvations

nirtzo   halayl   BORaych   tzofun   shulchon ōraych   kōraych   morc

uvshaym Adōnoy ekro.   וּבְשֵׁם יהוה אֶקְרָא.
and the Name of HASHEM I will invoke.

N'dorai La-dōnoy ashalaym,   נְדָרַי לַיהוה אֲשַׁלֵם,
My vows to HASHEM I will pay,

negdo no l'chol amō.   נֶגְדָה נָּא לְכָל עַמּוֹ.
in the presence, now, of His entire people.

Yokor b'aynay Adōnoy   יָקָר בְּעֵינֵי יהוה
hamovso lachasidov.   הַמָּוְתָה לַחֲסִידָיו.
Difficult in the eyes of HASHEM is the death of His devout ones.

Ono Adōnoy ki ani avdecho,   אָנָּה יהוה כִּי אֲנִי עַבְדֶּךָ,
Please, HASHEM — for I am Your servant,

ani avd'cho, ben amosecho,   אֲנִי עַבְדְּךָ, בֶּן אֲמָתֶךָ,
I am Your servant, son of Your handmaid —

pitachto l'mōsayroy.   פִּתַּחְתָּ לְמוֹסֵרָי.
You have released my bonds.

L'cho ezbach zevach tōdo,   לְךָ אֶזְבַּח זֶבַח תּוֹדָה,
To You I will sacrifice thanksgiving offerings,

uvshaym Adōnoy ekro.   וּבְשֵׁם יהוה אֶקְרָא.
and the Name of HASHEM I will invoke.

N'dorai La-dōnoy ashalaym,   נְדָרַי לַיהוה אֲשַׁלֵם,
My vows to HASHEM I will pay,

negdo no l'chol amō.   נֶגְדָה נָּא לְכָל עַמּוֹ.
in the presence, now, of His entire people.

B'chatzrōs bays Adōnoy,   בְּחַצְרוֹת בֵּית יהוה,
In the Courtyards of the House of HASHEM,

b'sōchaychi y'rusholo-yim,   בְּתוֹכֵכִי יְרוּשָׁלָיִם
in your midst, O Jerusalem,

hal'luyoh.   הַלְלוּיָהּ.
Praise God!

■   The nations are called upon to recognize God and worship Him.

HAL'LU es Adōnoy, kol gōyim,   הַלְלוּ אֶת יהוה, כָּל גּוֹיִם,
Praise HASHEM, all nations;

קָדֵּשׁ וּרְחַץ כַּרְפַּס יַחַץ מַגִּיד רָחְצָה מוֹצִיא מַ
...tzo   mōtzi   roch'tzo   magid   yachatz   karpas   ur'chatz   kadaysh

shab'chuhu kol ho-umim.　　　שַׁבְּחוּהוּ כָּל הָאֻמִּים.

praise Him, all the states!

ki govar olaynu chasdō,　　　כִּי גָבַר עָלֵינוּ חַסְדּוֹ,

For His kindness has overwhelmed us,

ve-emes Adōnoy l'ōlom　　　וֶאֱמֶת יהוה לְעוֹלָם,

and the truth of HASHEM is eternal,

hal'luyoh.　　　הַלְלוּיָהּ.

Praise God!

■ Not only the Kohanim and the rest of Israel, but all who fear God, must praise Him.

HŌDU La-dōnoy ki tōv,　　　**הוֹדוּ** לַיהוה כִּי טוֹב,

Give thanks to HASHEM for He is good;

ki l'ōlom chasdō.　　　כִּי לְעוֹלָם חַסְדּוֹ.

His kindness endures forever!

Yōmar no yisro-ayl,　　　יֹאמַר נָא יִשְׂרָאֵל,

Let Israel say now:

ki l'ōlom chasdō.　　　כִּי לְעוֹלָם חַסְדּוֹ.

His kindness endures forever!

Yōm'ru no vays aharōn,　　　יֹאמְרוּ נָא בֵית אַהֲרֹן,

Let the House of Aaron say now:

ki l'ōlom chasdō.　　　כִּי לְעוֹלָם חַסְדּוֹ.

His kindness endures forever!

Yōm'ru no yir-ay Adōnoy,　　　יֹאמְרוּ נָא יִרְאֵי יהוה,

Let those who fear HASHEM say now:

ki l'ōlom chasdō.　　　כִּי לְעוֹלָם חַסְדּוֹ.

His kindness endures forever!

■ "I shall not die," that is, I shall not act like the wicked who, devoid of positive contribution to this world, are considered as dead, even during their lifetime. "I shall live," in a meaningful way, by serving God.

MIN HAMAYTZAR korosi Yoh,　　　**מִן הַמֵּצַר** קָרָאתִי יָּהּ,

From the straits did I call upon God;

ononi vamerchov Yoh.　　　עָנָנִי בַמֶּרְחָב יָהּ.

God answered me with expansiveness.

Adōnoy li lō iro,　　　יהוה לִי לֹא אִירָא,

HASHEM is with me, I have no fear;

מַה יַּעֲשֶׂה לִי אָדָם.

ma ya-ase li odom.

how can man affect me?

יהוה לִי בְּעֹזְרָי,

Adōnoy li b'ōz'roy,

HASHEM is with me through my helpers;

וַאֲנִי אֶרְאֶה בְשׂנְאָי.

va-ani er-e v'sōn'oy.

therefore I can face my foes.

טוֹב לַחֲסוֹת בַּיהוה,
מִבְּטֹחַ בָּאָדָם.

Tōv la-chasōs Ba-dōnoy,
mib'tō-ach bo-odom.

It is better to take refuge in HASHEM than to rely on man.

טוֹב לַחֲסוֹת בַּיהוה,
מִבְּטֹחַ בִּנְדִיבִים.

Tōv la-chasōs Ba-dōnoy,
mib'tō-ach bindivim.

It is better to take refuge in HASHEM than to rely on nobles.

כָּל גּוֹיִם סְבָבוּנִי,

Kol gōyim s'vovuni,

All the nations surround me;

בְּשֵׁם יהוה כִּי אֲמִילַם.

b'shaym Adōnoy ki amilam.

in the Name of HASHEM I cut them down!

סַבּוּנִי גַם סְבָבוּנִי,

Sabuni gam s'vovuni,

They encircle me, they also surround me;

בְּשֵׁם יהוה כִּי אֲמִילַם.

b'shaym Adōnoy ki amilam.

in the Name of HASHEM, I cut them down!

סַבּוּנִי כִדְבֹרִים

Sabuni chidvōrim

They encircle me like bees,

דֹּעֲכוּ כְּאֵשׁ קוֹצִים,

dō-achu k'aysh kōtzim,

but they are extinguished as a fire does thorns;

בְּשֵׁם יהוה כִּי אֲמִילַם.

b'shaym Adōnoy ki amilam.

in the Name of HASHEM I cut them down!

דָּחֹה דְחִיתַנִי לִנְפֹּל,
וַיהוה עֲזָרָנִי.

Dochō d'chisani linpōl,
Va-dōnoy azoroni.

You pushed me hard that I might fall, but HASHEM assisted me.

עָזִּי וְזִמְרָת יָהּ,

Ozi v'zimros Yoh,

God is my might and my praise,

וַיְהִי לִי לִישׁוּעָה.

vai-hi li lishu-o.

and He was a salvation for me.

קַדֵּשׁ ׀ וּרְחַץ ׀ כַּרְפַּס ׀ יַחַץ ׀ מַגִּיד ׀ רָחְצָה ׀ מוֹצִיא מַ

ﬞtzo   mōtzi   Roch'tzo   magid   yachatz   karpas   ur'chatz   kadaysh

Kōl rino vishu-o,
 b'oholay tzadikim,

קוֹל רִנָּה וִישׁוּעָה,
בְּאָהֳלֵי צַדִּיקִים,

The sound of rejoicing and salvation is in the tents of the righteous:

Y'min Adōnoy ōso cho-yil.

יְמִין יהוה עֹשָׂה חָיִל.

"HASHEM's right hand does valiantly.

Y'min Adōnoy rōmaymo,

יְמִין יהוה רוֹמֵמָה,

HASHEM's right hand is raised triumphantly;

y'min Adōnoy ōso cho-yil.

יְמִין יהוה עֹשָׂה חָיִל.

HASHEM's right hand does valiantly!"

Lō omus ki echye,
 va-asapayr ma-asay Yoh.

לֹא אָמוּת כִּי אֶחְיֶה,
וַאֲסַפֵּר מַעֲשֵׂי יָהּ.

I shall not die! But I shall live and relate the deeds of God.

Yasōr yis'rani Yoh,
 v'lamo-ves lō n'sononi.

יַסֹּר יִסְּרַנִּי יָּהּ,
וְלַמָּוֶת לֹא נְתָנָנִי.

God has chastened me exceedingly, but He did not let me die.

Pischu li sha-aray tzedek,

פִּתְחוּ לִי שַׁעֲרֵי צֶדֶק,

Open for me the gates of righteousness,

ovō vom ō-de Yoh.

אָבֹא בָם אוֹדֶה יָהּ.

I will enter them and thank God.

Ze ha-sha-ar La-dōnoy,

זֶה הַשַּׁעַר לַיהוה,

This is the gate of HASHEM;

tzadikim yovō-u vō.

צַדִּיקִים יָבֹאוּ בוֹ.

the righteous shall enter through it.

Ōd'cho ki anisoni,
 vat'hi li li-shu-o.

אוֹדְךָ כִּי עֲנִיתָנִי,
וַתְּהִי לִי לִישׁוּעָה.

I thank You for You have answered me and become my salvation.

Ōd'cho ki anisoni,
 vat'hi li li-shu-o.

אוֹדְךָ כִּי עֲנִיתָנִי,
וַתְּהִי לִי לִישׁוּעָה.

I thank You for You have answered me and become my salvation.

Even mo-asu habōnim,
 ho-y'so l'rōsh pino.

אֶבֶן מָאֲסוּ הַבּוֹנִים,
הָיְתָה לְרֹאשׁ פִּנָּה.

The stone the builders despised has become the cornerstone.

nirtzo   halayl   boraych   tzofun   shulchon ōraych   kōraych   moró

Even mo-asu habōnim,
ho-y'so l'rōsh pino.

אֶבֶן מָאֲסוּ הַבּוֹנִים,
הָיְתָה לְרֹאשׁ פִּנָּה.

The stone the builders despised has become the cornerstone.

May-ays Adōnoy ho-y'so zōs,
hi niflos b'aynaynu.

מֵאֵת יהוה הָיְתָה זֹּאת,
הִיא נִפְלָאת בְּעֵינֵינוּ.

This emanated from HASHEM; it is wondrous in our eyes.

May-ays Adōnoy ho-y'so zōs,
hi niflos b'aynaynu.

מֵאֵת יהוה הָיְתָה זֹּאת,
הִיא נִפְלָאת בְּעֵינֵינוּ.

This emanated from HASHEM; it is wondrous in our eyes.

Ze ha-yōm oso Adōnoy,
nogilo v'nism'cho vō.

זֶה הַיּוֹם עָשָׂה יהוה,
נָגִילָה וְנִשְׂמְחָה בוֹ.

This is the day HASHEM has made; let us rejoice and be glad on it.

Ze ha-yōm oso Adōnoy
nogilo v'nism'cho vō.

זֶה הַיּוֹם עָשָׂה יהוה,
נָגִילָה וְנִשְׂמְחָה בוֹ.

This is the day HASHEM has made; let us rejoice and be glad on it.

ONO Adōnoy hōshi-o no.

אָנָּא יהוה הוֹשִׁיעָה נָּא.

Please, HASHEM, save now!

Ono Adōnoy hōshi-o no.

אָנָּא יהוה הוֹשִׁיעָה נָּא.

Please, HASHEM, save now!

Ono Adōnoy hatzlicho no.

אָנָּא יהוה הַצְלִיחָה נָּא.

Please, HASHEM, bring success now!

Ono Adōnoy hatzlicho no.

אָנָּא יהוה הַצְלִיחָה נָּא.

Please, HASHEM, bring success now.

BORUCH HABO b'shaym
Adōnoy,

בָּרוּךְ הַבָּא בְּשֵׁם
יהוה,

Blessed is he who comes in the Name of HASHEM;

bayrachnuchem mibays Adōnoy.

בֵּרַכְנוּכֶם מִבֵּית יהוה.

we bless you from the House of HASHEM.

Boruch habo b'shaym Adōnoy,

בָּרוּךְ הַבָּא בְּשֵׁם יהוה,

Blessed is he who comes in the Name of HASHEM;

bayrachnuchem mibays Adōnoy.

בֵּרַכְנוּכֶם מִבֵּית יהוה.

we bless you from the House of HASHEM.

Ayl Adōnoy va-yo-er lonu,

אֵל יהוה וַיָּאֶר לָנוּ,

HASHEM is God, He illuminated for us;

isru chag ba-avōsim,

אִסְרוּ חַג בַּעֲבֹתִים,

bind the festival-offering with cords

ad karnōs hamizbay-ach.

עַד קַרְנוֹת הַמִּזְבֵּחַ.

until the corners of the Altar.

Ayl Adōnoy va-yo-er lonu,

אֵל יהוה וַיָּאֶר לָנוּ,

HASHEM is God, He illuminated for us;

isru chag ba-avōsim,

אִסְרוּ חַג בַּעֲבֹתִים,

bind the festival-offering with cords

ad karnōs hamizbay-ach.

עַד קַרְנוֹת הַמִּזְבֵּחַ.

until the corners of the Altar.

Ayli ato v'ōdeko,
   Elōhai arōm'meko.

אֵלִי אַתָּה וְאוֹדֶךָּ,
אֱלֹהַי אֲרוֹמְמֶךָּ.

You are my God, and I will thank You; my God, I will exalt You.

Ayli ato v'ōdeko,
   Elōhai arōm'meko.

אֵלִי אַתָּה וְאוֹדֶךָּ,
אֱלֹהַי אֲרוֹמְמֶךָּ.

You are my God, and I will thank You; my God, I will exalt You.

Hōdu La-dōnoy ki tōv,

הוֹדוּ לַיהוה כִּי טוֹב,

Give thanks to HASHEM, for He is good;

ki l'ōlom chasdō.

כִּי לְעוֹלָם חַסְדּוֹ.

His kindness endures forever.

Hōdu La-dōnoy ki tōv,

הוֹדוּ לַיהוה כִּי טוֹב,

Give thanks to HASHEM, for He is good;

ki l'ōlom chasdō.

כִּי לְעוֹלָם חַסְדּוֹ.

His kindness endures forever.

Y'HAL'LUCHO Adōnoy Elōhaynu

יְהַלְלוּךָ יהוה אֱלֹהֵינוּ

kol ma-asecho,

כָּל מַעֲשֶׂיךָ,

All Your works shall praise You, HASHEM, our God;

vachasidecho tzadikim
ōsay r'tzōnecho,

וַחֲסִידֶיךָ צַדִּיקִים
עוֹשֵׂי רְצוֹנֶךָ,

and Your devout ones, the righteous who do Your will,

nirtzo   halayl   Boraych   tzofun   shulchon ōraych   kōraych   morō

v'chol am'cho bays yisro-ayl
וְכָל עַמְּךָ בֵּית יִשְׂרָאֵל
and Your entire people, the House of Israel,

b'rino yōdu vi-vor'chu
בְּרִנָּה יוֹדוּ וִיבָרְכוּ
with glad song will thank, bless,

vi-shab'chu vifo-aru virōm'mu
וִישַׁבְּחוּ וִיפָאֲרוּ וִירוֹמְמוּ
praise, glorify, exalt,

v'ya-aritzu v'yakdishu v'yamlichu
וְיַעֲרִיצוּ וְיַקְדִּישׁוּ וְיַמְלִיכוּ
extol, sanctify and proclaim the sovereignty

es shimcho malkaynu.
אֶת שִׁמְךָ מַלְכֵּנוּ.
of Your Name, our King.

Ki l'cho tōv l'hōdōs
כִּי לְךָ טוֹב לְהוֹדוֹת
For to You it is fitting to give thanks,

ulshimcho no-e l'zamayr,
וּלְשִׁמְךָ נָאֶה לְזַמֵּר,
and unto Your Name it is proper to sing praises,

ki may-ōlom v'ad ōlom ato Ayl.
כִּי מֵעוֹלָם וְעַד עוֹלָם אַתָּה אֵל.
for from this world to the World to Come You are God.

■ In twenty-six verses, representing the twenty-six generations from Creation until the Exodus and the giving of the Torah, the Psalmist recapitulates the history of the world up to the Jews' entry into the Holy Land. For each occurrence we thank God for His enduring kindness.

HŌDU La-dōnoy ki tōv,
הוֹדוּ לַיהוה כִּי טוֹב,
Give thanks to HASHEM for He is good,

ki l'ōlom chasdō.
כִּי לְעוֹלָם חַסְדּוֹ.
for His kindness endures forever.

Hōdu Laylōhay ho-elōhim,
הוֹדוּ לֵאלֹהֵי הָאֱלֹהִים,
Give thanks to the God of the heavenly powers,

ki l'ōlom chasdō.
כִּי לְעוֹלָם חַסְדּוֹ.
for His kindness endures forever.

Hōdu La-adōnay ho-adōnim,
הוֹדוּ לַאֲדֹנֵי הָאֲדֹנִים,
Give thanks to the Lord of the lords,

ki l'ōlom chasdō.
כִּי לְעוֹלָם חַסְדּוֹ.
for His kindness endures forever.

L'ōsay niflo-ōs g'dōlōs l'vadō,
לְעֹשֵׂה נִפְלָאוֹת גְּדֹלוֹת לְבַדּוֹ,
To Him Who alone performs great wonders,

קַדֵּשׁ וּרְחַץ כַּרְפַּס יַחַץ מַגִּיד רָחְצָה מוֹצִיא מַצָּ
tzo mōtzi roch'tzo magid yachatz karpas ur'chatz kadaysh

ki l'ōlom chasdō.

כִּי לְעוֹלָם חַסְדּוֹ.

for His kindness endures forever.

L'ōsay ha-shoma-yim bisvuno,

לְעֹשֵׂה הַשָּׁמַיִם בִּתְבוּנָה,

To Him Who makes the heavens with understanding,

ki l'ōlom chasdō.

כִּי לְעוֹלָם חַסְדּוֹ.

for His kindness endures forever.

L'rōka ho-oretz al hamo-yim,

לְרוֹקַע הָאָרֶץ עַל הַמָּיִם,

To Him Who spreads out the earth upon the waters,

ki l'ōlom chasdō.

כִּי לְעוֹלָם חַסְדּוֹ.

for His kindness endures forever.

L'ōsay ōrim g'dōlim,

לְעֹשֵׂה אוֹרִים גְּדֹלִים,

To Him Who makes great lights,

ki l'ōlom chasdō.

כִּי לְעוֹלָם חַסְדּוֹ.

for His kindness endures forever.

Es hashemesh l'memsheles ba-yōm,

אֶת הַשֶּׁמֶשׁ לְמֶמְשֶׁלֶת בַּיּוֹם,

The sun for the reign of the day,

ki l'ōlom chasdō.

כִּי לְעוֹלָם חַסְדּוֹ.

for His kindness endures forever.

Es ha-yoray-ach v'chōchovim
l'memsh'lōs baloylo,

אֶת הַיָּרֵחַ וְכוֹכָבִים
לְמֶמְשְׁלוֹת בַּלָּיְלָה,

The moon and the stars for the reign of the night,

ki l'ōlom chasdō.

כִּי לְעוֹלָם חַסְדּוֹ.

for His kindness endures forever.

L'makay mitzra-yim bivchōrayhem,

לְמַכֵּה מִצְרַיִם בִּבְכוֹרֵיהֶם,

To Him Who smote Egypt through their firstborn,

ki l'ōlom chasdō.

כִּי לְעוֹלָם חַסְדּוֹ.

for His kindness endures forever.

Va-yōtzay yisro-ayl mitōchom,

וַיּוֹצֵא יִשְׂרָאֵל מִתּוֹכָם,

And brought Israel forth from their midst,

ki l'ōlom chasdō.

כִּי לְעוֹלָם חַסְדּוֹ.

for His kindness endures forever.

B'yod chazoko u-vizrō-a n'tu-yo,

בְּיָד חֲזָקָה וּבִזְרוֹעַ נְטוּיָה,

With strong hand and outstretched arm,

ki l'ōlom chasdō.

כִּי לְעוֹלָם חַסְדּוֹ.

for His kindness endures forever.

L'gōzayr yam suf ligzorim,

לְגֹזֵר יַם סוּף לִגְזָרִים,

To Him Who divided the Sea of Reeds into parts,

ki l'ōlom chasdō.

כִּי לְעוֹלָם חַסְדּוֹ.

for His kindness endures forever.

V'he-evir yisro-ayl b'sōchō,

וְהֶעֱבִיר יִשְׂרָאֵל בְּתוֹכוֹ,

And caused Israel to pass through it,

ki l'ōlom chasdō.

כִּי לְעוֹלָם חַסְדּוֹ.

for His kindness endures forever.

V'ni-ayr par-ō v'chaylō v'yam suf,

וְנִעֵר פַּרְעֹה וְחֵילוֹ בְיַם סוּף,

And threw Pharaoh and his army into the Sea of Reeds,

ki l'ōlom chasdō.

כִּי לְעוֹלָם חַסְדּוֹ.

for His kindness endures forever.

L'mōlich amō bamidbor,

לְמוֹלִיךְ עַמּוֹ בַּמִּדְבָּר,

To Him Who led His people through the wilderness,

ki l'ōlom chasdō.

כִּי לְעוֹלָם חַסְדּוֹ.

for His kindness endures forever.

L'makay m'lochim g'dōlim,

לְמַכֵּה מְלָכִים גְּדֹלִים,

To Him Who smote great kings,

ki l'ōlom chasdō.

כִּי לְעוֹלָם חַסְדּוֹ.

for His kindness endures forever.

Va-yaharōg m'lochim adirim,

וַיַּהֲרֹג מְלָכִים אַדִּירִים,

And slew mighty kings,

ki l'ōlom chasdō.

כִּי לְעוֹלָם חַסְדּוֹ.

for His kindness endures forever.

L'sichōn melech ho-emōri,

לְסִיחוֹן מֶלֶךְ הָאֱמֹרִי,

Sichon, king of the Emorites,

ki l'ōlom chasdō.

כִּי לְעוֹלָם חַסְדּוֹ.

for His kindness endures forever.

Ul-ōg melech ha-boshon,

וּלְעוֹג מֶלֶךְ הַבָּשָׁן,

And Og, king of Bashan,

ki l'ōlom chasdō.

כִּי לְעוֹלָם חַסְדּוֹ.

for His kindness endures forever.

קַדֵּשׁ וּרְחַץ כַּרְפַּס יַחַץ מַגִּיד רָחְצָה מוֹצִיא מַ

ōtzo mōtzi roch'tzo magīd yachatz karpas ur'chatz kadaysh

V'nosan artzom l'nachalo, וְנָתַן אַרְצָם לְנַחֲלָה,

And presented their land as a heritage,

ki l'ōlom chasdō. כִּי לְעוֹלָם חַסְדּוֹ.

for His kindness endures forever.

Nachalo l'yisro-ayl avdō, נַחֲלָה לְיִשְׂרָאֵל עַבְדּוֹ,

A heritage for Israel, His servant,

ki l'ōlom chasdō. כִּי לְעוֹלָם חַסְדּוֹ.

for His kindness endures forever.

Sheb'shiflaynu zochar lonu, שֶׁבְּשִׁפְלֵנוּ זָכַר לָנוּ,

In our lowliness He remembered us,

ki l'ōlom chasdō. כִּי לְעוֹלָם חַסְדּוֹ.

for His kindness endures forever.

Va-yifr'kaynu mi-tzoraynu, וַיִּפְרְקֵנוּ מִצָּרֵינוּ,

And He released us from our tormentors,

ki l'ōlom chasdō. כִּי לְעוֹלָם חַסְדּוֹ.

for His kindness endures forever.

Nōsayn lechem l'chol bosor, נֹתֵן לֶחֶם לְכָל בָּשָׂר,

He gives nourishment to all flesh,

ki l'ōlom chasdō. כִּי לְעוֹלָם חַסְדּוֹ.

for His kindness endures forever.

Hōdu l'Ayl ha-shomo-yim, הוֹדוּ לְאֵל הַשָּׁמָיִם,

Give thanks to God of the heavens,

ki l'ōlom chasdō. כִּי לְעוֹלָם חַסְדּוֹ.

for His kindness endures forever.

■ We praise and thank God for His universal beneficence; He is the First, He is the Last; He is Eternal — God of all creatures, of all generations, of all humanity. But in the last analysis we acknowledge our allegiance to Him, not because we understand His achievements, but for Himself alone. His greatness, not merely His largess, is the source of our adoration and love for Him.

NISHMAS kol chai נִשְׁמַת כָּל חַי

The soul of every living being

t'voraych es shimcho תְּבָרֵךְ אֶת שִׁמְךָ

shall bless Your Name,

Adōnoy Elōhaynu, יהוה אֱלֹהֵינוּ,

HASHEM, our God;

nirtzo halayl boraych tzofun shulchon ōraych kōraych moror

v'ru-ach kol bosor

וְרוּחַ כָּל בָּשָׂר

the spirit of all flesh

t'fo-ayr usrōmaym
zichr'cho malkaynu tomid.

תְּפָאֵר וּתְרוֹמֵם
זִכְרְךָ מַלְכֵּנוּ תָּמִיד.

shall always glorify and exalt Your remembrance, our King.

Min ho-ōlom v'ad ho-ōlom
ato Ayl.

מִן הָעוֹלָם וְעַד הָעוֹלָם
אַתָּה אֵל,

From this world to the World to Come, You are God,

umi-bal-odecho ayn lonu melech
gō-ayl u-mōshi-a.

וּמִבַּלְעָדֶיךָ אֵין לָנוּ מֶלֶךְ
גּוֹאֵל וּמוֹשִׁיעַ.

and other than You we have no king, redeemer or savior.

Pōde u-matzil umfarnays
umrachaym

פּוֹדֶה וּמַצִּיל וּמְפַרְנֵס
וּמְרַחֵם

Liberator, Rescuer, Sustainer and Merciful One

b'chol ays tzoro v'tzuko,

בְּכָל עֵת צָרָה וְצוּקָה,

in every time of distress and anguish,

ayn lonu melech elo oto.

אֵין לָנוּ מֶלֶךְ אֶלָּא אָתָּה.

we have no king but You!

Elōhay horishōnim
v'ho-acharōnim,

אֱלֹהֵי הָרִאשׁוֹנִים
וְהָאַחֲרוֹנִים,

God of the first and of the last,

Elō-ha kol b'riyōs,

אֱלוֹהַּ כָּל בְּרִיּוֹת,

God of all creatures,

adōn kol tōlodōs,

אֲדוֹן כָּל תּוֹלָדוֹת,

Master of all generations,

ham'hulol b'rōv hatishbochōs,

הַמְהֻלָּל בְּרֹב הַתִּשְׁבָּחוֹת,

Who is extolled through a multitude of praises,

ham'nahayg ōlomō b'chesed

הַמְנַהֵג עוֹלָמוֹ בְּחֶסֶד

Who guides His world with kindness

uvri-yōsov b'rachamim.

וּבְרִיּוֹתָיו בְּרַחֲמִים.

and His creatures with mercy.

Va-dōnoy lō yonum v'lō yishon.

וַיהוה לֹא יָנוּם וְלֹא יִישָׁן.

HASHEM neither slumbers nor sleeps.

Ham'ōrayr y'shaynim, הַמְעוֹרֵר יְשֵׁנִים,
He Who rouses the sleepers,

v'hamaykitz nirdomim, וְהַמֵּקִיץ נִרְדָּמִים,
Who awakens the slumberers,

v'hamaysi-ach il'mim, וְהַמֵּשִׂיחַ אִלְּמִים,
Who makes the mute speak,

v'hamatir asurim, וְהַמַּתִּיר אֲסוּרִים,
Who releases the bound,

v'hasōmaych nōf'lim, וְהַסּוֹמֵךְ נוֹפְלִים,
Who supports the fallen,

v'hazōkayf k'fufim, וְהַזּוֹקֵף כְּפוּפִים,
and Who straightens the bent —

L'cho l'vad'cho a-nachnu mōdim. לְךָ לְבַדְּךָ אֲנַחְנוּ מוֹדִים.
to You alone we give thanks.

Ilu finu molay shiro ka-yom, אִלּוּ פִינוּ מָלֵא שִׁירָה כַּיָּם,
Were our mouth as full of song as the sea,

ulshōnaynu rino kahamōn galov, וּלְשׁוֹנֵנוּ רִנָּה כַּהֲמוֹן גַּלָּיו,
and our tongue as full of joyous song as its multitude of waves,

v'sifsōsaynu shevach וְשִׂפְתוֹתֵינוּ שֶׁבַח
k'merchavay roki-a, כְּמֶרְחֲבֵי רָקִיעַ,
and our lips as full of praise as the breadth of the heavens,

v'aynaynu m'irōs וְעֵינֵינוּ מְאִירוֹת
ka-shemesh v'cha-yoray-ach, כַּשֶּׁמֶשׁ וְכַיָּרֵחַ,
and our eyes as brilliant as the sun and the moon,

v'yodaynu f'rusōs וְיָדֵינוּ פְרוּשׂוֹת
k'nishray shomo-yim, כְּנִשְׁרֵי שָׁמָיִם,
and our hands as outspread as eagles of the sky

v'raglaynu kalōs ko-a-yolōs, וְרַגְלֵינוּ קַלּוֹת כָּאַיָּלוֹת,
and our feet as swift as hinds —

ayn anachnu maspikim אֵין אֲנַחְנוּ מַסְפִּיקִים
l'hōdōs l'cho לְהוֹדוֹת לָךְ,
we still could not thank You sufficiently,

nirtzo halayl bōraych tzofun shulchon ōraych kōraych mor

Adōnoy Elōhaynu

יהוה אֱלֹהֵינוּ

Vaylōhay avōsaynu,

וֵאלֹהֵי אֲבוֹתֵינוּ,

HASHEM, our God and God of our forefathers,

ulvoraych es sh'mecho

וּלְבָרֵךְ אֶת שְׁמֶךָ

and to bless Your Name

al achas may-olef

עַל אַחַת מֵאֶלֶף

elef alfay alofim

אֶלֶף אַלְפֵי אֲלָפִים

for even one of the thousand thousand, thousands of thousands

v'ribay r'vovōs p'omim hatōvōs

וְרִבֵּי רְבָבוֹת פְּעָמִים הַטּוֹבוֹת

and myriad myriads of favors

she-osiso im avōsaynu v'imonu.

שֶׁעָשִׂיתָ עִם אֲבוֹתֵינוּ וְעִמָּנוּ.

that You performed for our ancestors and for us.

Mimitzra-yim g'altonu

מִמִּצְרַיִם גְּאַלְתָּנוּ

You redeemed us from Egypt,

Adōnoy Elōhaynu,

יהוה אֱלֹהֵינוּ,

HASHEM, our God,

u-mibays avodim p'disonu.

וּמִבֵּית עֲבָדִים פְּדִיתָנוּ.

and liberated us from the house of bondage.

B'ro-ov zantonu,

בְּרָעָב זַנְתָּנוּ,

In famine You nourished us

uvsovo kilkaltonu,

וּבְשָׂבָע כִּלְכַּלְתָּנוּ,

and in plenty You sustained us.

maycherev hitzaltonu,

מֵחֶרֶב הִצַּלְתָּנוּ,

From sword You saved us;

u-midever milat-tonu,

וּמִדֶּבֶר מִלַּטְתָּנוּ,

from plague You let us escape;

u-maycholo-yim ro-im v'ne-emonim dilisonu.

וּמֵחֳלָיִם רָעִים וְנֶאֱמָנִים דִּלִּיתָנוּ.

and from severe and enduring diseases You spared us.

Ad hayno azorunu rachamecho,

עַד הֵנָּה עֲזָרוּנוּ רַחֲמֶיךָ,

Until now Your mercy has helped us,

v'lō azovunu chasodecho

וְלֹא עֲזָבוּנוּ חֲסָדֶיךָ.

and Your kindness has not forsaken us.

קַדֵּשׁ וּרְחַץ כַּרְפַּס יַחַץ מַגִּיד רָחְצָה מוֹצִיא מַ

atzo mōtzi roch'tzo magid yachatz karpas ur'chatz kadaysh

V'al tit'shaynu Adōnoy Elōhaynu   וְאַל תִּטְּשֵׁנוּ יהוה אֱלֹהֵינוּ
    lonetzach.   לָנֶצַח.

Do not abandon us, HASHEM, our God, forever.

Al kayn   עַל כֵּן

Therefore,

ayvorim shepilagto bonu,   אֵבָרִים שֶׁפִּלַּגְתָּ בָּנוּ,

the organs that You set within us,

v'ru-ach unshomo   וְרוּחַ וּנְשָׁמָה
    shenofachto b'apaynu,   שֶׁנָּפַחְתָּ בְּאַפֵּינוּ,

and the spirit and soul that You breathed into our nostrils,

v'loshōn asher samto b'finu,   וְלָשׁוֹן אֲשֶׁר שַׂמְתָּ בְּפִינוּ,

and the tongue that You placed in our mouth —

hayn haym yōdu vivor'chu   הֵן הֵם יוֹדוּ וִיבָרְכוּ

all of them shall thank and bless

vishab'chu vifo-aru virōm'mu   וִישַׁבְּחוּ וִיפָאֲרוּ וִירוֹמְמוּ

and praise and glorify and exalt

v'ya-aritzu v'yakdishu   וְיַעֲרִיצוּ וְיַקְדִּישׁוּ

and revere and sanctify

v'yamlichu es shimcho malkaynu.   וְיַמְלִיכוּ אֶת שִׁמְךָ מַלְכֵּנוּ.

and declare the sovereignty of Your Name, our King.

Ki chol pe l'cho yōde,   כִּי כָל פֶּה לְךָ יוֹדֶה,

For every mouth shall offer thanks to You;

v'chol loshōn l'cho si-shova,   וְכָל לָשׁוֹן לְךָ תִשָּׁבַע,

every tongue shall vow allegiance to You;

v'chol berech l'cho sichra,   וְכָל בֶּרֶךְ לְךָ תִכְרַע,

every knee shall bend to You;

v'chol kōmo l'fonecho sishta-chave,   וְכָל קוֹמָה לְפָנֶיךָ תִשְׁתַּחֲוֶה,

every erect spine shall prostrate itself before You;

v'chol l'vovōs yiro-ucho,   וְכָל לְבָבוֹת יִירָאוּךְ,

all hearts shall fear You,

v'chol kerev uchlo-yōs   וְכָל קֶרֶב וּכְלָיוֹת
    y'zam'ru lishmecho,   יְזַמְּרוּ לִשְׁמֶךָ,

and all innermost feelings and thoughts shall sing praises to Your name,

nirtzo   halayl   вoraych   tzofun   shulchon ōraych   kōraych   mor kadovor shekosuv:

כַּדָּבָר שֶׁכָּתוּב:

as it is written:

Kol atzmōsai tōmarno,

כָּל עַצְמֹתַי תֹּאמַרְנָה,

"All my bones shall say:

Adōnoy mi chomōcho,

יהוה מִי כָמוֹךָ,

'HASHEM, who is like You?'

matzil oni maychozok mimenu,

מַצִּיל עָנִי מֵחָזָק מִמֶּנּוּ,

You save the poor man from one stronger than he,

v'oni v'evyōn migōz'lō.

וְעָנִי וְאֶבְיוֹן מִגֹּזְלוֹ.

the poor and destitute from one who would rob him."

Mi yidme loch,
  u-mi yishve loch,

מִי יִדְמֶה לָּךְ,
וּמִי יִשְׁוֶה לָּךְ,

Who is like unto You? Who is equal to You?

u-mi ya-aroch loch.

וּמִי יַעֲרָךְ לָךְ.

Who can be compared to You?

Ho-Ayl hagodōl hagibōr
  v'hanōro,

הָאֵל הַגָּדוֹל הַגִּבּוֹר
וְהַנּוֹרָא,

O great, mighty and awesome God,

Ayl elyōn,

אֵל עֶלְיוֹן,

the supreme God,

kōnay shoma-yim vo-oretz.

קֹנֵה שָׁמַיִם וָאָרֶץ.

Creator of heaven and earth.

N'halelcho unshabaychacho
  unfo-ercho

נְהַלֶּלְךָ וּנְשַׁבֵּחֲךָ
וּנְפָאֶרְךָ

We shall laud, praise and glorify You

unvoraych es shaym kodshecho,

וּנְבָרֵךְ אֶת שֵׁם קָדְשֶׁךָ,

and bless Your holy Name,

ko-omur: L'dovid,

כָּאָמוּר: לְדָוִד,

as it is said: "Of David:

bor'chi nafshi es Adōnoy,

בָּרְכִי נַפְשִׁי אֶת יהוה,

Bless HASHEM, O my soul,

v'chol k'rovai es shaym kodshō.

וְכָל קְרָבַי אֶת שֵׁם קָדְשׁוֹ.

and let all my innermost being bless His holy Name!"

קַדֵּשׁ וּרְחַץ כַּרְפַּס יַחַץ מַגִּיד רָחְצָה מוֹצִיא מַ

otzo   mōtzi   roch'tzo   magid   yachatz   karpas   ur'chatz   kadaysh

HO-AYL b'sa-atzumōs u-zecho,   הָאֵל בְּתַעֲצֻמוֹת עֻזֶּךָ,

O God, in the omnipotence of Your strength,

hagodōl bichvōd sh'mecho,   הַגָּדוֹל בִּכְבוֹד שְׁמֶךָ,

great in the glory of Your Name,

hagibōr lonetzach   הַגִּבּוֹר לָנֶצַח

    v'hanōro b'nōr'ōsecho.   וְהַנּוֹרָא בְּנוֹרְאוֹתֶיךָ.

mighty forever and awesome through Your awesome deeds.

Hamelech ha-yōshayv   הַמֶּלֶךְ הַיּוֹשֵׁב

    al kisay rom v'niso.   עַל כִּסֵּא רָם וְנִשָּׂא.

O King enthroned upon a high and lofty throne!

SHŌCHAYN AD   שׁוֹכֵן עַד

He Who abides forever,

morōm v'kodōsh sh'mō.   מָרוֹם וְקָדוֹשׁ שְׁמוֹ.

exalted and holy is His Name.

V'chosuv: Ran'nu tzadikim   וְכָתוּב: רַנְּנוּ צַדִּיקִים

    Ba-dōnoy   בַּיהוה

And it is written: "Sing joyfully, O righteous, before HASHEM;

lai-shorim novo s'hilo.   לַיְשָׁרִים נָאוָה תְהִלָּה.

for the upright, praise is fitting."

B'fi y'shorim tis-halol,   בְּפִי **יְ**שָׁרִים תִּתְהַלָּל,

By the mouth of the upright shall You be lauded;

Uvdivray tzadikim tisborach,   וּבְדִבְרֵי **צַ**דִּיקִים תִּתְבָּרַךְ,

by the words of the righteous shall You be blessed;

U-vilshōn chasidim tisrōmom,   וּבִלְשׁוֹן **חֲ**סִידִים תִּתְרוֹמָם,

by the tongue of the devout shall You be exalted;

Uvkerev k'dōshim tiskadosh.   וּבְקֶרֶב **קְ**דוֹשִׁים תִּתְקַדָּשׁ.

and amid the holy shall You be sanctified.

UVMAK-HALŌS riv'vōs   וּבְמַקְהֲלוֹת רִבְבוֹת

    am'cho bays yisro-ayl,   עַמְּךָ בֵּית יִשְׂרָאֵל,

And in the assemblies of the myriads of Your people, the House of Israel,

b'rino yispo-ar shimcho malkaynu   בְּרִנָּה יִתְפָּאַר שִׁמְךָ מַלְכֵּנוּ

with joyous song shall Your Name be glorified, our King,

nirtzo   haLayl   BORaych   tzofun   shulchon ōraych   kōraych   morō

b'chol dōr vodōr. בְּכָל דּוֹר וָדוֹר.

throughout every generation.

Shekayn chōvas kol ha-y'tzurim, שֶׁכֵּן חוֹבַת כָּל הַיְּצוּרִים,

For such is the duty of all creatures —

l'fonecho Adōnoy Elōhaynu לְפָנֶיךָ יהוה אֱלֹהֵינוּ
Vaylōhay avōsaynu, וֵאלֹהֵי אֲבוֹתֵינוּ,

before You, HASHEM, our God and the God of our forefathers,

l'hōdōs l'halayl l'shabay-ach לְהוֹדוֹת לְהַלֵּל לְשַׁבֵּחַ

to thank, laud, praise,

l'fo-ayr l'rōmaym l'hadayr לְפָאֵר לְרוֹמֵם לְהַדֵּר

glorify, exalt, adore,

l'voraych l'alay ul-kalays, לְבָרֵךְ לְעַלֵּה וּלְקַלֵּס,

bless, raise high and sing praises —

al kol divray shirōs עַל כָּל דִּבְרֵי שִׁירוֹת
v'sishb'chōs וְתִשְׁבָּחוֹת

even beyond all expressions of the songs and praises

dovid ben yishai דָּוִד בֶּן יִשַׁי
avd'cho m'shichecho. עַבְדְּךָ מְשִׁיחֶךָ.

of David the son of Jesse, Your servant, Your anointed.

YISHTABACH shimcho lo-ad יִשְׁתַּבַּח שִׁמְךָ לָעַד
malkaynu, מַלְכֵּנוּ,

May Your Name be praised forever — our King,

ho-Ayl hamelech hagodōl הָאֵל הַמֶּלֶךְ הַגָּדוֹל
v'hakodōsh, וְהַקָּדוֹשׁ,

the God, the great and holy King —

ba-shoma-yim uvo-oretz. בַּשָּׁמַיִם וּבָאָרֶץ.

in heaven and on earth.

Ki l'cho no-e Adōnoy Elōhaynu כִּי לְךָ נָאֶה יהוה אֱלֹהֵינוּ
Vaylōhay avōsaynu, וֵאלֹהֵי אֲבוֹתֵינוּ,

Because for You is fitting — O HASHEM, our God and the God of our forefathers —

shir ushvocho, halayl v'zimro, שִׁיר וּשְׁבָחָה, הַלֵּל וְזִמְרָה,

song and praise, lauding and hymns,

קַדֵּשׁ וּרְחַץ כַּרְפַּס יַחַץ מַגִּיד רָחְצָה מוֹצִיא מַצ
ōtzo mōtzi rōch'tzo magid yachatz karpas ur'chatz kadaysh

ōz u-memsholo,   עֹז וּמֶמְשָׁלָה,

  netzach, g'dulo ugvuro,   נֶצַח גְּדֻלָּה וּגְבוּרָה,

power and dominion, triumph, greatness and strength,

t'hilo v'sif-eres,   תְּהִלָּה וְתִפְאֶרֶת,

  k'dusho u-malchus,   קְדֻשָּׁה וּמַלְכוּת,

praise and splendor, holiness and sovereignty,

b'rochōs v'hōdo-ōs   בְּרָכוֹת וְהוֹדָאוֹת

  may-ato v'ad ōlom.   מֵעַתָּה וְעַד עוֹלָם.

blessings and thanksgivings from this time and forever.

Boruch ato Adōnoy,   בָּרוּךְ אַתָּה יהוה,

Blessed are You, HASHEM,

Ayl melech godōl batishbochōs,   אֵל מֶלֶךְ גָּדוֹל בַּתִּשְׁבָּחוֹת,

God, King exalted through praises,

Ayl hahōdo-ōs, adōn haniflo-ōs,   אֵל הַהוֹדָאוֹת, אֲדוֹן הַנִּפְלָאוֹת,

God of thanksgivings, Master of wonders,

habōchayr b'shiray zimro,   הַבּוֹחֵר בְּשִׁירֵי זִמְרָה,

Who chooses musical songs of praise —

melech Ayl chay ho-ōlomim.   מֶלֶךְ אֵל חֵי הָעוֹלָמִים.

King, God, Life-giver of the world.

THE BLESSING OVER WINE IS RECITED AND THE FOURTH CUP IS DRUNK WHILE RECLINING
TO THE LEFT SIDE. IT IS PREFERABLE THAT THE ENTIRE CUP BE DRUNK.

BORUCH ato Adōnoy   **בָּרוּךְ** אַתָּה יהוה

Blessed are You, HASHEM

Elōhaynu melech ho-ōlom   אֱלֹהֵינוּ מֶלֶךְ הָעוֹלָם,

our God, King of the universe,

bōray p'riy hagofen.   בּוֹרֵא פְּרִי הַגָּפֶן.

Who creates the fruit of the vine.

AFTER DRINKING THE FOURTH CUP, THE CONCLUDING BLESSING IS RECITED.

BORUCH ato Adōnoy,   **בָּרוּךְ** אַתָּה יהוה

Blessed are You, HASHEM,

Elōhaynu melech ho-ōlom,   אֱלֹהֵינוּ מֶלֶךְ הָעוֹלָם,

our God, King of the universe,

al hagefen v'al p'ri hagefen,   עַל הַגֶּפֶן וְעַל פְּרִי הַגֶּפֶן,

for the vine and the fruit of the vine

v'al t'nuvas haso-de,   וְעַל תְּנוּבַת הַשָּׂדֶה,

and for the produce of the field;

v'al eretz chemdo   וְעַל אֶרֶץ חֶמְדָּה

tōvo urchovo,   טוֹבָה וּרְחָבָה,

for the desirable, good and spacious Land

sherotziso v'hinchalto   שֶׁרָצִיתָ וְהִנְחַלְתָּ

la-avōsaynu,   לַאֲבוֹתֵינוּ,

that You were pleased to give our forefathers as a heritage,

le-echōl mipiryoh   לֶאֱכוֹל מִפִּרְיָהּ

to eat of its fruit

v'lisbō-a mituvoh.   וְלִשְׂבּוֹעַ מִטּוּבָהּ.

and to be satisfied with its goodness.

Rachaym no Adōnoy Elōhaynu   רַחֵם נָא יהוה אֱלֹהֵינוּ

Have mercy, we beg You, HASHEM, our God,

al yisro-ayl amecho,   עַל יִשְׂרָאֵל עַמֶּךָ,

on Israel, Your people;

v'al y'rushola-yim i-recho,   וְעַל יְרוּשָׁלַיִם עִירֶךָ,

on Jerusalem, Your city;

v'al tzi-yōn mishkan k'vōdecho,   וְעַל צִיּוֹן מִשְׁכַּן כְּבוֹדֶךָ,

on Zion, the resting place of Your glory;

v'al mizb'checho v'al haycholecho.   וְעַל מִזְבְּחֶךָ וְעַל הֵיכָלֶךָ.

on Your Altar and on Your Temple.

Uvnay y'rushola-yim ir hakōdesh   וּבְנֵה יְרוּשָׁלַיִם עִיר הַקֹּדֶשׁ

Rebuild Jerusalem, the Holy City,

bimhayro v'yomaynu,   בִּמְהֵרָה בְיָמֵינוּ,

speedily in our days.

v'ha-alaynu l'sōchoh,   וְהַעֲלֵנוּ לְתוֹכָהּ,

Bring us up into it

v'sam'chaynu b'vinyonoh,   וְשַׂמְּחֵנוּ בְּבִנְיָנָהּ,

and gladden us in its rebuilding

קַדֵּשׁ וּרְחַץ כַּרְפַּס יַחַץ מַגִּיד רָחְצָה מוֹצִיא מַצָּ

atzo   mōtzi   roch'tzo   magid   yachatz   karpas   ur'chatz   kadaysh

v'nōchal mipiryoh,

and let us eat from its fruit

וְנאכַל מִפִּרְיָה,

v'nisba mituvoh,

and be satisfied with its goodness

וְנִשְׂבַּע מִטּוּבָהּ,

unvorech'cho oleho

and bless You upon it

וּנְבָרֶכְךָ עָלֶיהָ

bikdusho uvtohoro.

in holiness and purity.

בִּקְדֻשָּׁה וּבְטָהֳרָה.

ON THE SABBATH ADD:

Urtzay v'ha-chalitzaynu

And be pleased to let us rest

וּרְצֵה וְהַחֲלִיצֵנוּ

b'yōm ha-shabos ha-ze.

on this Sabbath day.

בְּיוֹם הַשַּׁבָּת הַזֶּה.

V'sam'chaynu

And gladden us

וְשַׂמְּחֵנוּ

b'yōm chag hamatzōs ha-ze.

on this day of the Festival of Matzos.

בְּיוֹם חַג הַמַּצּוֹת הַזֶּה.

Ki ato Adōnoy

For You, HASHEM,

כִּי אַתָּה יהוה

tōv u-maytiv lakōl,

are good and do good to all

טוֹב וּמֵטִיב לַכֹּל,

v'nō-de lecho al ho-oretz

and we thank You for the Land

וְנוֹדֶה לְךָ עַל הָאָרֶץ

IF THE WINE IS FROM ISRAEL, RECITE THE WORD IN BRACKETS
INSTEAD OF THE PRECEDING WORD.

v'al p'ri hagefen [gafnoh],

and for the fruit of the [its] vine

וְעַל פְּרִי הַגֶּפֶן [גַפְנָהּ].

Boruch ato Adōnoy,

Blessed are You, HASHEM,

בָּרוּךְ אַתָּה יהוה,

al ho-oretz

for the Land

עַל הָאָרֶץ

v'al p'ri hagefen [gafnoh],

and for the fruit of the [its] vine.

וְעַל פְּרִי הַגֶּפֶן [גַפְנָהּ].

� nⁱrtzo   haLayl   Boraych   tzofun   shulchon ōraych   kōraych   mor

נרצה / NIRTZO

■ In accordance with the verse, "Let my tongue adhere to my palate . . . if I fail to elevate Jerusalem above my foremost joy!" we pray that our reenactment of the past redemption sets the stage for the future redemption, that we may celebrate next year's Seder in the Holy City.

CHASAL sidur pesach   חֲסַל סִדּוּר פֶּסַח

The order of the Pesach service is now completed

k'hilchosō,   כְּהִלְכָתוֹ,

in accordance with its laws,

K'chol mishpotō v'chukosō.   כְּכָל מִשְׁפָּטוֹ וְחֻקָּתוֹ.

with all its ordinances and statutes.

Ka-asher zochinu l'sadayr ōsō,   כַּאֲשֶׁר זָכִינוּ לְסַדֵּר אוֹתוֹ.

Just as we were privileged to arrange it,

kayn nizke la-asōsō.   כֵּן נִזְכֶּה לַעֲשׂוֹתוֹ.

so may we merit to perform it.

Zoch shōchayn m'ōno.   זָךְ שׁוֹכֵן מְעוֹנָה.

O Pure One, Who dwells on high,

Kōmaym k'hal adas mi mono.   קוֹמֵם קְהַל עֲדַת מִי מָנָה.

raise up the countless congregation!

B'korōv nahayl nitay chano.   בְּקָרוֹב נַהֵל נִטְעֵי כַנָּה.

Soon, lead the offshoots of Your plants,

p'duyim l'tziyōn b'rino.   פְּדוּיִם לְצִיּוֹן בְּרִנָּה.

redeemed, to Zion with glad song.

L'SHONO HABO-O   לְשָׁנָה הַבָּאָה

Next year

BIRUSHOLO-YIM.   בִּירוּשָׁלָיִם.

in Jerusalem!

קַדֵּשׁ וּרְחַץ כַּרְפַּס יַחַץ מַגִּיד רׇחְצָה מוֹצִיא מַצ
atzo   mōtzi   roch'tzo   magid   yachatz   karpas   ur'chatz   kadaysh

ON THE FIRST NIGHT RECITE THE FOLLOWING.
ON THE SECOND NIGHT CONTINUE ON PAGE 122.

■ We begin by mentioning many of the miracles God performed at night: Abraham defeated the four kings; Abimelech was judged for kidnapping Sarah; Laban was warned, in a dream, not to harm Jacob; Jacob defeated Esau's guardian angel; the Egyptian firstborn died and their wealth was lost; Sisera's army was destroyed; Sennacherib and his armies fell dead; Nebuchadnezzar's statue and its pedestal broke; Daniel interpreted Nebuchadnezzar's dreams; Belshazzar was killed just after Daniel disclosed the secret of "the handwriting on the wall"; and Ahasuerus' sleep was disturbed, leading to Haman's downfall.

But what will be the outcome of this long exile night? We beseech God: May You tread on those who oppress us. May light shine for the righteous, and darkness enshroud the wicked. Hasten the time of redemption for Your nation, for Your city. Let the darkness of exile be brightened by the light of day.

UV'CHAYN vai-hi bachatzi halai-lo.

וּבְכֵן וַיְהִי בַּחֲצִי הַלַּיְלָה.

It came to pass at midnight.

Oz rōv nisim hiflayso balai-lo.

אָז רוֹב נִסִּים הִפְלֵאתָ בַּלַּיְלָה.

You have of old, performed many wonders by night.

B'rōsh ashmōres ze halai-lo.

בְּרֹאשׁ אַשְׁמוֹרֶת זֶה הַלַּיְלָה.

At the beginning of the first watch of this night.

Gayr tzedek nitzachtō

גֵּר צֶדֶק נִצַּחְתּוֹ

To the righteous convert (Abraham) You gave victory

k'nechelak lō lai-lo.

כְּנֶחֱלַק לוֹ לַיְלָה.

when it was divided for him the night.

Vai-hi bachatzi halai-lo.

וַיְהִי בַּחֲצִי הַלַּיְלָה.

It came to pass at midnight.

Danto melech g'ror bachalōm halai-lo.

דַּנְתָּ מֶלֶךְ גְּרָר בַּחֲלוֹם הַלַּיְלָה.

You judged the king of Gerar (Abimelech with death) in a dream by night.

Hifchadto arami b'emesh lai-lo.

הִפְחַדְתָּ אֲרַמִּי בְּאֶמֶשׁ לַיְלָה.

You frightened the Aramean (Laban) in the dark of night.

Vayosar yisro-ayl l'maloch

וַיָּשַׂר יִשְׂרָאֵל לְמַלְאָךְ

Israel (Jacob) fought with an angel

vayuchal lō lai-lo.

וַיּוּכַל לוֹ לַיְלָה.

and overcame him by night.

Vai-hi bachatzi halai-lo.

וַיְהִי בַּחֲצִי הַלַּיְלָה.

It came to pass at midnight.

Zera b'chōray fasrōs

זֶרַע בְּכוֹרֵי פַתְרוֹס

The first-born children of the Egyptian

mochatzto bachatzi halai-lo.

מָחַצְתָּ בַּחֲצִי הַלַּיְלָה.

You crushed at midnight.

Chaylom lō motz'u

חֵילָם לֹא מָצְאוּ

Their host they found not

b'kumom balai-lo.

בְּקוּמָם בַּלַּיְלָה.

when they arose at night.

Tisas n'gid charōshes siliso

טִיסַת נְגִיד חֲרוֹשֶׁת סִלִּיתָ

You swept away the army of the prince of Charoshes (Sisra)

b'chōch'vay lai-lo.

בְּכוֹכְבֵי לַיְלָה.

with the stars of night.

Vai-hi bachatzi halai-lo.

וַיְהִי בַּחֲצִי הַלַּיְלָה.

It came to pass at midnight.

Yo-atz m'chorayf l'nōfayf,

יָעַץ מְחָרֵף לְנוֹפֵף,

The blasphemer (Sennacherib) had planned to raise his hand against Jerusalem.

ivuy hōvashto f'gorov balai-lo.

אִוּי הוֹבַשְׁתָּ פְגָרָיו בַּלַּיְלָה.

You withered his corpses by night.

Kora bayl umatzovō

כָּרַע בֵּל וּמַצָּבוֹ

[The idol] Bel was overturned, with its pedestal,

b'ishōn lai-lo.

בְּאִישׁוֹן לַיְלָה.

in the darkness of the night.

L'ish chamudōs

לְאִישׁ חֲמוּדוֹת

To the man of Your delights (Daniel)

niglo roz chazōs lai-lo.

נִגְלָה רָז חֲזוֹת לַיְלָה.

was revealed the mystery of the visions at night.

Vai-hi bachatzi halai-lo.

וַיְהִי בַּחֲצִי הַלַּיְלָה.

It came to pass at midnight.

Mishtakayr bichlay kōdesh

מִשְׁתַּכֵּר בִּכְלֵי קֹדֶשׁ

He who caroused from the holy vessels (Belshazzar)

קַדֵּשׁ וּרְחַץ כַּרְפַּס יַחַץ מַגִּיד רָחְצָה מוֹצִיא מַצָּ

atzo   mōtzi   Roch'tzo   magid   yachatz   karpas   ur'chatz   kadaysh

neherag bō balai-lo.   נֶהֱרַג בּוֹ בַּלַּיְלָה.

was killed on that very night.

Nōsha mibōr aroyōs   נוֹשַׁע מִבּוֹר אֲרָיוֹת

From the lions' den was rescued he (Daniel)

pōsayr bi-asusay lai-lo.   פּוֹתֵר בְּעִתוּתֵי לָיְלָה.

who interpreted the meaning of the "terrors" of the night.

Sino notar agogi   שִׂנְאָה נָטַר אֲגָגִי

The Aggagite (Haman) nursed hatred in his heart

v'chosav s'forim balai-lo.   וְכָתַב סְפָרִים בַּלַּיְלָה.

and wrote decrees at night.

Vai-hi bachatzi halai-lo.   וַיְהִי בַּחֲצִי הַלַּיְלָה.

It came to pass at midnight.

Ōrarto nitzchacho olov   עוֹרַרְתָּ נִצְחֲךָ עָלָיו

You began Your triumph over him (Ahasuerus)

b'neded sh'nas lai-lo.   בְּנֶדֶד שְׁנַת לָיְלָה.

when You disturbed his sleep at night.

Puro sidrōch l'shōmayr   פּוּרָה תִדְרוֹךְ לְשׁוֹמֵר

Trample the wine-press to help those who ask the watchman,

ma milai-lo.   מַה מִלַּיְלָה.

"What of the long night?"

Tzorach kashōmayr v'soch   צָרַח כַּשּׁוֹמֵר וְשָׂח

He will exclaim, like a watchman, and say,

oso vōker v'gam lai-lo.   אָתָא בֹקֶר וְגַם לָיְלָה.

"Morning shall come after this night."

Vai-hi bachatzi halai-lo.   וַיְהִי בַּחֲצִי הַלַּיְלָה.

It came to pass at midnight.

Korayv yōm   קָרֵב יוֹם

Hasten the day (of the Messiah),

asher hu lō yōm v'lō lai-lo.   אֲשֶׁר הוּא לֹא יוֹם וְלֹא לָיְלָה.

that is neither day nor night.

Rom hōda   רָם הוֹדַע

Most High, make known

ki l'cho hayōm af l'cho halai-lo.   כִּי לְךָ הַיּוֹם אַף לְךָ הַלָּיְלָה.

that Yours is the day as well as the night.

Shōm'rim hafkayd l'ir'cho   שׁוֹמְרִים הַפְקֵד לְעִירֶךָ

Appoint watchmen to Your city (Jerusalem)

kol hayōm v'chol halai-lo.   כָּל הַיּוֹם וְכָל הַלָּיְלָה.

by day and by night.

To-ir k'ōr yōm cheshkas lai-lo.   תָּאִיר כְּאוֹר יוֹם חֶשְׁכַּת לַיְלָה.

Brighten like the light of day, the darkness of the night.

Vai-hi bachatzi halai-lo.   וַיְהִי בַּחֲצִי הַלָּיְלָה.

It came to pass at midnight.

ON THE FIRST NIGHT CONTINUE ON PAGE 125.
ON THE SECOND NIGHT RECITE THE FOLLOWING:

■ You exhibited Your awesome might many times on Pesach: You visited Abraham and foretold Isaac's birth; overturned Sodom but saved Lot; granted Joshua victory over Jericho; and delivered Midian into Gideon's hands. Additionally, the defeats of Sennacherib, Belshazzar, and Haman all occurred on Pesach.
May you bring the downfall of Edom, show the strength which You showed on the night of Pesach, and redeem us as in days of old.

UV'CHAYN va-amartem   וּבְכֵן וַאֲמַרְתֶּם

zevach pesach.   זֶבַח פֶּסַח:

And you shall say: This is the feast of Passover.

Ōmetz g'vurōsecho   אֹמֶץ גְּבוּרוֹתֶיךָ

The strength of Your powers

hiflayso bapesach.   הִפְלֵאתָ בַּפֶּסַח.

You wondrously displayed on Passover.

B'rōsh kol mō-adōs   בְּרֹאשׁ כָּל מוֹעֲדוֹת

Above all festivals

nisayso pesach.   נִשֵּׂאתָ פֶּסַח.

You elevated Passover.

Giliso l'ezrochi   גִּלִּיתָ לְאֶזְרָחִי

To the Oriental (Abraham) You revealed

chatzōs layl pesach.   חֲצוֹת לֵיל פֶּסַח.

the future midnight of Passover.

Va-amartem zevach pesach.   וַאֲמַרְתֶּם זֶבַח פֶּסַח.

And you shall say: This is the feast of Passover.

D'losov dofakto   דְּלָתָיו דָּפַקְתָּ

At his (Abraham's) door You knocked

k'chōm hayōm bapesach.   כְּחֹם הַיּוֹם בַּפֶּסַח.

in the midday heat on Passover;

Hisid nōtz'tzim   הִסְעִיד נוֹצְצִים

He satiated the angels of God

ugōs matzōs bapesach.   עֲגוֹת מַצּוֹת בַּפֶּסַח.

with matzoh-cakes on Passover.

V'el habokor rotz   וְאֶל הַבָּקָר רָץ

And he ran to the cattle —

zaycher l'shōr erech pesach.   זֵכֶר לְשׁוֹר עֶרֶךְ פֶּסַח.

symbolic of the sacrificial beast of Passover.

Va-amartem zevach pesach.   וַאֲמַרְתֶּם זֶבַח פֶּסַח.

And you shall say: This is the feast of Passover.

Zō-amu s'dōmim   זוֹעֲמוּ סְדוֹמִים

The men of Sodom provoked God

v'lōhatu bo-aysh bapesach.   וְלוֹהֲטוּ בָּאֵשׁ בַּפֶּסַח.

and were devoured by fire on Passover;

Chulatz lōt mayhem   חֻלַּץ לוֹט מֵהֶם

Lot was saved from among them —

umatzōs ofo b'kaytz pesach.   וּמַצּוֹת אָפָה בְּקֵץ פֶּסַח.

he had baked matzos at the time of Passover.

Titayso admas mōf v'nōf   טִאטֵאתָ אַדְמַת מוֹף וְנוֹף

You swept clean the soil of Moph and Noph (Egyptian provinces)

b'ovr'cho bapesach.   בְּעָבְרְךָ בַּפֶּסַח.

when You passed through them on Passover.

Va-amartem zevach pesach.   וַאֲמַרְתֶּם זֶבַח פֶּסַח.

And you shall say: This is the feast of Passover.

Yoh rōsh kol ōn mochatzto   יָהּ רֹאשׁ כָּל אוֹן מָחַצְתָּ

You, God, destroyed all the firstborn (of Egypt)

b'layl shimur pesach.   בְּלֵיל שִׁמּוּר פֶּסַח.

on the watchful night of Passover.

nirtzo   halayl   boraych   tzofun   shulchon ōraych   kōraych   morō

Kabir al bayn b'chōr posachto   כַּבִּיר עַל בֵּן בְּכוֹר פָּסַחְתָּ

Master, Your firstborn, You passed over

b'dam pesach   בְּדַם פֶּסַח.

by merit of the blood of Passover,

L'vilti tays mashchis   לְבִלְתִּי תֵּת מַשְׁחִית

Because of it You did not let destruction

lovō bifsochai bapesach.   לָבֹא בִּפְתָחַי בַּפֶּסַח.

enter my doors on Passover.

Va-amartem zevach pesach.   וַאֲמַרְתֶּם זֶבַח פֶּסַח.

And you shall say: This is the feast of Passover.

M'sugeres sugoro b'itōsay fesach.   מְסֻגֶּרֶת סֻגָּרָה בְּעִתּוֹתֵי פֶּסַח.

The beleaguered city (Jericho) was besieged on Passover.

Nishm'do midyon   נִשְׁמְדָה מִדְיָן

Midian was destroyed

bitzlil s'ōray ōmer pesach.   בִּצְלִיל שְׂעוֹרֵי עֹמֶר פֶּסַח.

with a barley cake, from the Omer of Passover.

Sōr'fu mishmanay pul v'lud   שׂוֹרְפוּ מִשְׁמַנֵּי פוּל וְלוּד

The nobles of Pul and Lud (Assyria) were consumed

bikad y'kōd pesach.   בִּיקַד יְקוֹד פֶּסַח.

in a mighty conflagration on Passover.

Va-amartem zevach pesach.   וַאֲמַרְתֶּם זֶבַח פֶּסַח.

And you shall say: This is the feast of Passover.

Ōd hayōm b'nōv la-amōd   עוֹד הַיּוֹם בְּנֹב לַעֲמוֹד

He (Sennacherib) would have stood on that day in Nob,

ad go-o ōnas pesach.   עַד גָּעָה עוֹנַת פֶּסַח.

but for the advent of Passover.

Pas yad kos'vo   פַּס יַד כָּתְבָה

A hand wrote,

l'ka-akay-a tzul bapesach.   לְקַעֲקֵעַ צוּל בַּפֶּסַח.

inscribing the destruction of Zul (Babylon) on Passover,

Tzofō hatzofis   צָפֹה הַצָּפִית

As the watch was set,

oróch hashulchon bapesach.

עָרוֹךְ הַשֻּׁלְחָן בַּפֶּסַח.

the royal table was decked, on Passover.

Va-amartem zevach pesach.

וַאֲמַרְתֶּם זֶבַח פֶּסַח.

And you shall say: This is the feast of Passover.

Kohol kin'so hadaso

קָהָל כִּנְּסָה הֲדַסָּה

Hadassah (Esther) gathered a congregation

tzōm l'shalaysh bapesach.

צוֹם לְשַׁלֵּשׁ בַּפֶּסַח.

for a three-day fast on Passover.

Rōsh mibays rosho mochatzto

רֹאשׁ מִבֵּית רָשָׁע מָחַצְתָּ

You caused the head of the evil clan (Haman) to be hanged

b'aytz chamishim bapesach.

בְּעֵץ חֲמִשִּׁים בַּפֶּסַח.

from a gallows fifty cubits high, on Passover.

Sh'tay ayle rega tovi l'utzis
bapesach.

שְׁתֵּי אֵלֶּה רֶגַע תָּבִיא לְעוּצִית
בַּפֶּסַח.

Double misfortune You will bring in a moment upon Utsis (Edom) on Passover;

To-ōz yod'cho v'sorum y'min'cho

תָּעֹז יָדְךָ וְתָרוּם יְמִינֶךָ

May Your hand be strong, Your right hand exalted,

k'layl hiskadaysh chag pesach.

כְּלֵיל הִתְקַדֵּשׁ חַג פֶּסַח.

as on that night when You made holy the festival of Passover,

Va-amartem zevach pesach.

וַאֲמַרְתֶּם זֶבַח פֶּסַח.

And you shall say: This is the feast of Passover.

ON BOTH NIGHTS CONTINUE HERE:

■ We cannot possibly list all of God's praises for He and His praises are infinite. It has become the practice to use an alphabetical ordering of praise, as if to say, "We praise You in every way which starts with the letter aleph, or beis, or gimmel . . . from the beginning of the alphabet to the end."

KI LŌ NO-E. KI LŌ YO-E:

כִּי לוֹ נָאֶה, כִּי לוֹ יָאֶה:

To Him praise is due! To Him praise is fitting!

Adir bimlucho.

אַדִּיר בִּמְלוּכָה,

Powerful in kingship,

Bochur kahalocho.

בָּחוּר כַּהֲלָכָה,

Perfectly distinguished,

G'dudov yōm'ru lō.

גְּדוּדָיו יֹאמְרוּ לוֹ,

His companies of angels say to him:

L'cho ulcho. L'cho ki l'cho.
L'cho af l'cho.

לְךָ וּלְךָ, לְךָ כִּי לְךָ,
לְךָ אַף לְךָ,

Yours and only Yours; Yours, yes Yours; Yours, surely Yours;

L'cho Adōnoy hamamlocho.

לְךָ יהוה הַמַּמְלָכָה,

Yours, HASHEM, is the sovereignty.

Ki lō no-e. Ki lō yo-e.

כִּי לוֹ נָאֶה, כִּי לוֹ יָאֶה.

To Him praise is due. To Him praise is fitting.

Dogul bimlucho.

דָּגוּל בִּמְלוּכָה,

Supreme in kingship,

Hodur kahalocho.

הָדוּר כַּהֲלָכָה,

Perfectly glorious,

Vosikov yōm'ru lō.

וָתִיקָיו יֹאמְרוּ לוֹ,

His faithful say to Him:

L'cho ulcho. L'cho ki l'cho.
L'cho af l'cho.

לְךָ וּלְךָ, לְךָ כִּי לְךָ,
לְךָ אַף לְךָ,

Yours and only Yours; Yours, yes Yours; Yours, surely Yours;

L'cho Adōnoy hamamlocho.

לְךָ יהוה הַמַּמְלָכָה,

Yours, HASHEM, is the sovereignty.

Ki lō no-e. Ki lō yo-e.

כִּי לוֹ נָאֶה, כִּי לוֹ יָאֶה.

To Him praise is due. To Him praise is fitting.

Zakay bimlucho.

זַכַּאי בִּמְלוּכָה,

Pure in kingship,

Chosin kahalocho.

חָסִין כַּהֲלָכָה,

Perfectly mighty,

Tafs'rov yōm'ru lō.

טַפְסְרָיו יֹאמְרוּ לוֹ,

His angels say unto Him:

L'cho ulcho. L'cho ki l'cho.
L'cho af l'cho.

לְךָ וּלְךָ, לְךָ כִּי לְךָ,
לְךָ אַף לְךָ,

Yours and only Yours; Yours, yes Yours; Yours, surely Yours;

L'cho Adōnoy hamamlocho.

לְךָ יהוה הַמַּמְלָכָה,

Yours, HASHEM, is the sovereignty.

קַדֵּשׁ וּרְחַץ כַּרְפַּס יַחַץ מַגִּיד רָחְצָה מוֹצִיא מַצ

atzo   mōtzi   roch'tzo   magid   yachatz   karpas   ur'chatz   kadaysh

Ki lō no-e. Ki lō yo-e.　　　　כִּי לוֹ נָאֶה, כִּי לוֹ יָאֶה.

To Him praise is due. To Him praise is fitting.

Yochid bimlucho　　　　יָחִיד בִּמְלוּכָה,

Alone in kingship,

kabir kahalocho.　　　　כַּבִּיר כַּהֲלָכָה,

perfectly omnipotent,

Limudov yōm'ru lō.　　　　לִמּוּדָיו יֹאמְרוּ לוֹ,

His scholars say unto Him:

L'cho ulcho. L'cho ki l'cho.　　　　לְךָ וּלְךָ, לְךָ כִּי לְךָ,
　L'cho af l'cho.　　　　לְךָ אַף לְךָ,

Yours and only Yours; Yours, yes Yours; Yours, surely Yours;

L'cho Adōnoy hamamlocho.　　　　לְךָ יהוה הַמַּמְלָכָה,

Yours, HASHEM, is the sovereignty.

Ki lō no-e. Ki lō yo-e.　　　　כִּי לוֹ נָאֶה, כִּי לוֹ יָאֶה.

To Him praise is due. To Him praise is fitting.

Mōshayl bimlucho.　　　　מוֹשֵׁל בִּמְלוּכָה,

Commanding in kingship,

Nōro kahalocho.　　　　נוֹרָא כַּהֲלָכָה,

perfectly awesome,

S'vivov yōm'ru lō.　　　　סְבִיבָיו יֹאמְרוּ לוֹ,

His surrounding (angels) say unto Him:

L'cho ulcho. L'cho ki l'cho.　　　　לְךָ וּלְךָ, לְךָ כִּי לְךָ,
　L'cho af l'cho.　　　　לְךָ אַף לְךָ,

Yours and only Yours; Yours, yes Yours; Yours, surely Yours;

L'cho Adōnoy hamamlocho.　　　　לְךָ יהוה הַמַּמְלָכָה,

Yours, HASHEM, is the sovereignty.

Ki lō no-e. Ki lō yo-e.　　　　כִּי לוֹ נָאֶה, כִּי לוֹ יָאֶה.

To Him praise is due. To Him praise is fitting.

Onov bimlucho.　　　　עָנָיו בִּמְלוּכָה,

Gentle in Kingship,

Pōde kahalocho.　　　　פּוֹדֶה כַּהֲלָכָה,

perfectly the Redeemer,

nirtzo　halayl　boraych　tzofun　shulchon ōraych　kōraych　morō

Tzadikov yōm'ru lō.

צַדִּיקָיו יֹאמְרוּ לוֹ,

His righteous ones say to Him:

L'cho ulcho. L'cho ki l'cho.
L'cho af l'cho.

לְךָ וּלְךָ, לְךָ כִּי לְךָ,
לְךָ אַף לְךָ,

Yours and only Yours; Yours, yes Yours; Yours, surely Yours;

L'cho Adōnoy hamamlocho.

לְךָ יהוה הַמַּמְלָכָה,

Yours, HASHEM, is the sovereignty.

Ki lō no-e. Ki lō yo-e.

כִּי לוֹ נָאֶה, כִּי לוֹ יָאֶה.

To Him praise is due. To Him praise is fitting.

Kodōsh bimlucho.

קָדוֹשׁ בִּמְלוּכָה,

Holy in kingship,

Rachum kahalocho.

רַחוּם כַּהֲלָכָה,

perfectly merciful,

Shinanov yōm'ru lō.

שִׁנְאַנָּיו יֹאמְרוּ לוֹ,

His troops of angels say unto Him:

L'cho ulcho. L'cho ki l'cho.
L'cho af l'cho.

לְךָ וּלְךָ, לְךָ כִּי לְךָ,
לְךָ אַף לְךָ,

Yours and only Yours; Yours, yes Yours; Yours, surely Yours;

L'cho Adōnoy hamamlocho.

לְךָ יהוה הַמַּמְלָכָה,

Yours, HASHEM, is the sovereignty.

Ki lō no-e. Ki lō yo-e.

כִּי לוֹ נָאֶה, כִּי לוֹ יָאֶה.

To Him praise is due. To Him praise is fitting.

Takif bimlucho.

תַּקִּיף בִּמְלוּכָה,

Almighty in kingship.

Tōmaych kahalocho.

תּוֹמֵךְ כַּהֲלָכָה,

perfectly sustaining,

T'mimov yōm'ru lō.

תְּמִימָיו יֹאמְרוּ לוֹ,

His perfect ones say to Him:

L'cho ulcho. L'cho ki l'cho.
L'cho af l'cho.

לְךָ וּלְךָ, לְךָ כִּי לְךָ,
לְךָ אַף לְךָ,

Yours and only Yours; Yours, yes Yours; Yours, surely Yours;

L'cho Adōnoy hamamlocho.

לְךָ יהוה הַמַּמְלָכָה,

Yours, HASHEM, is the sovereignty.

קַדֵּשׁ וּרְחַץ כַּרְפַּס יַחַץ מַגִּיד רָחְצָה מוֹצִיא מ

zo mōtzi roch'tzo magio yachatz karpas ur'chatz kadaysh

Ki lō no-e. Ki lō yo-e.   כִּי לוֹ נָאֶה, כִּי לוֹ יָאֶה.

To Him praise is due. To Him praise is fitting.

■ This hymn conveys our fervent desire for the Messianic age and the rebuilt Temple. The Sages teach that the Third Temple will not be built by man but will descend from heaven at the time of the redemption. For this reason we ask that "He soon rebuild His House."

ADIR HU.   אַדִּיר הוּא

He is most mighty,

Yivne vaysō b'korōv.   יִבְנֶה בֵיתוֹ בְּקָרוֹב,

may He soon rebuild His House,

Bimhayro, bimhayro   בִּמְהֵרָה, בִּמְהֵרָה,

speedily, yes speedily,

b'yomaynu b'korōv.   בְּיָמֵינוּ בְּקָרוֹב.

in our days, soon.

Ayl b'nay, Ayl b'nay.   אֵל בְּנֵה, אֵל בְּנֵה,

Rebuild, God, rebuild God,

B'nay vays'cho b'korōv.   בְּנֵה בֵיתְךָ בְּקָרוֹב.

rebuild Your House soon!

Bochur hu. Godōl hu.   בָּחוּר הוּא. גָּדוֹל הוּא.
    Dogul hu.   דָּגוּל הוּא.

He is distinguished, He is great, He is exalted,

Yivne vaysō b'korōv.   יִבְנֶה בֵיתוֹ בְּקָרוֹב,

may He soon rebuild His House,

Bimhayro, bimhayro   בִּמְהֵרָה, בִּמְהֵרָה,

speedily, yes speedily,

b'yomaynu b'korōv.   בְּיָמֵינוּ בְּקָרוֹב.

in our days, soon.

Ayl b'nay, Ayl b'nay.   אֵל בְּנֵה, אֵל בְּנֵה,

Rebuild, God, rebuild God,

B'nay vays'cho b'korōv.   בְּנֵה בֵיתְךָ בְּקָרוֹב.

rebuild Your House soon!

Hodur hu. Vosik hu.   הָדוּר הוּא. וָתִיק הוּא.
    Zakai hu. Chosid hu.   זַכַּאי הוּא. חָסִיד הוּא.

He is all-glorious, He is faithful, He is faultless, He is righteous,

Yivne vaysō b'korōv.

יִבְנֶה בֵיתוֹ בְּקָרוֹב,

may He soon rebuild His House,

Bimhayro, bimhayro

בִּמְהֵרָה, בִּמְהֵרָה,

speedily, yes speedily,

b'yomaynu b'korōv.

בְּיָמֵינוּ בְּקָרוֹב.

in our days, soon.

Ayl b'nay, Ayl b'nay.

אֵל בְּנֵה, אֵל בְּנֵה,

Rebuild, God, rebuild God,

B'nay vays'cho b'korōv.

בְּנֵה בֵיתְךָ בְּקָרוֹב.

rebuild Your House soon!

Tohōr hu. Yochid hu.

טָהוֹר הוּא. יָחִיד הוּא.

  Kabir hu. Lomud hu.

כַּבִּיר הוּא. לָמוּד הוּא.

He is pure, He is unique, He is powerful, He is wise,

Melech hu. Nōro hu.

מֶלֶךְ הוּא. נוֹרָא הוּא.

  Sagiv hu. Izuz hu.

סַגִּיב הוּא. עִזּוּז הוּא.

He is King, He is glorious, He is sublime, He is all-powerful,

Pōde hu. Tzadik hu.

פּוֹדֶה הוּא. צַדִּיק הוּא.

He is the Redeemer, He is the all-righteous,

Yivne vaysō b'korōv.

יִבְנֶה בֵיתוֹ בְּקָרוֹב,

may He soon rebuild His House,

Bimhayro, bimhayro

בִּמְהֵרָה, בִּמְהֵרָה,

speedily, yes speedily,

b'yomaynu b'korōv.

בְּיָמֵינוּ בְּקָרוֹב.

in our days, soon.

Ayl b'nay, Ayl b'nay.

אֵל בְּנֵה, אֵל בְּנֵה,

Rebuild, God, rebuild God,

B'nay vayscho b'korōv.

בְּנֵה בֵיתְךָ בְּקָרוֹב.

rebuild Your House soon!

Kodōsh hu. Rachum hu.

קָדוֹשׁ הוּא. רַחוּם הוּא.

  Shadai hu. Takif hu.

שַׁדַּי הוּא. תַּקִּיף הוּא.

He is holy, He is compassionate, He is Almighty, He is omnipotent,

Yivneh vaysō b'korōv.

יִבְנֶה בֵיתוֹ בְּקָרוֹב,

may He soon rebuild His House,

קַדֵּשׁ וּרְחַץ כַּרְפַּס יַחַץ מַגִּיד רָחְצָה מוֹצִיא מַצָּ

atzo   mōtzi   roch'tzo   magid   yachatz   karpas   ur'chatz   kadaysh

Bimhayro, bimhayro

בִּמְהֵרָה, בִּמְהֵרָה,

speedily, yes speedily,

b'yomaynu b'korōv.

בְּיָמֵינוּ בְּקָרוֹב.

in our days, soon.

Ayl b'nay, Ayl b'nay.

אֵל בְּנֵה, אֵל בְּנֵה,

Rebuild, God, rebuild God,

B'nay vays'cho b'korōv.

בְּנֵה בֵיתְךָ בְּקָרוֹב.

rebuild Your House soon!

■ This hymn, which counts from one to thirteen, alludes to the merits
for which our ancestors were redeemed from Egypt.
They believed in the One God . . .

ECHOD MI YŌDAY-A.　　　אֶחָד מִי יוֹדֵעַ?

Who knows one?

Echod ani yōday-a.

אֶחָד אֲנִי יוֹדֵעַ.

I know one;

Echod Elōhaynu
　shebashoma-yim uvo-oretz.

אֶחָד אֱלֹהֵינוּ
שֶׁבַּשָּׁמַיִם וּבָאָרֶץ.

one is our God, in heaven and on earth.

■ and were eager to accept the two Tablets.

SH'NAYIM MI YŌDAY-A.　　שְׁנַיִם מִי יוֹדֵעַ?

Who knows two?

Sh'nayim ani yōday-a.

שְׁנַיִם אֲנִי יוֹדֵעַ.

I know two;

Sh'nay luchōs hab'ris.

שְׁנֵי לֻחוֹת הַבְּרִית,

two are the tablets of the Covenant;

Echod Elōhaynu
　shebashoma-yim uvo-oretz.

אֶחָד אֱלֹהֵינוּ
שֶׁבַּשָּׁמַיִם וּבָאָרֶץ.

one is our God, in heaven and on earth.

■ God had promised the three Patriarchs — Abraham, Isaac, Jacob —
that He would redeem their children.

SH'LŌSHO MI YŌDAY-A.　　שְׁלֹשָׁה מִי יוֹדֵעַ?

Who knows three?

Sh'lōsho ani yōday-a.

שְׁלשָׁה אֲנִי יוֹדֵעַ.

I know three;

Sh'lōsho ovōs.

שְׁלשָׁה אָבוֹת,

three are the Patriarchs;

Sh'nay luchōs hab'ris.

שְׁנֵי לֻחוֹת הַבְּרִית,

two are the tablets of the Covenant;

Echod Elōhaynu

אֶחָד אֱלֹהֵינוּ

shebashoma-yim uvo-oretz.

שֶׁבַּשָּׁמַיִם וּבָאָרֶץ.

one is our God, in heaven and on earth

■ The Israelite women followed the way of modest righteousness taught them by the four Matriarchs — Sarah, Rebecca, Rachel, Leah.

ARBA MI YŌDAY-A.

אַרְבַּע מִי יוֹדֵעַ?

Who knows four?

Arba ani yōday-a.

אַרְבַּע אֲנִי יוֹדֵעַ.

I know four;

Arba imohōs.

אַרְבַּע אִמָּהוֹת,

four are the Matriarchs;

Sh'lōsho ovōs.

שְׁלשָׁה אָבוֹת,

three are the Patriarchs;

Sh'nay luchōs hab'ris.

שְׁנֵי לֻחוֹת הַבְּרִית,

two are the tablets of the Covenant;

Echod Elōhaynu

אֶחָד אֱלֹהֵינוּ

shebashoma-yim uvo-oretz.

שֶׁבַּשָּׁמַיִם וּבָאָרֶץ.

one is our God, in heaven and on earth.

■ The Israelites would soon accept the Five Books of Moses, which form the core of the Written Torah, as well as the Oral Torah comprising the six sections of the Mishnah.

CHAMISHO MI YŌDAY-A.

חֲמִשָּׁה מִי יוֹדֵעַ?

Who knows five?

Chamisho ani yōday-a.

חֲמִשָּׁה אֲנִי יוֹדֵעַ.

I know five;

Chamisho chum-shay sōro.

חֲמִשָּׁה חֻמְשֵׁי תוֹרָה,

five are the books of the Torah;

Arba imohōs. Sh'lōsho ovōs.

אַרְבַּע אִמָּהוֹת, שְׁלשָׁה אָבוֹת,

four are the Matriarchs; three are the Patriarchs;

atzo   mōtzi   roch'tzo   magid   yachatz   karpas   ur'chatz   kadaysh   קַדֵּשׁ וּרְחַץ כַּרְפַּס יַחַץ מַגִּיד רָחְצָה מוֹצִיא מַצָּ

Sh'nay luchōs hab'ris.
שְׁנֵי לֻחוֹת הַבְּרִית,

two are the tablets of the Covenant;

Echod Elōhaynu
אֶחָד אֱלֹהֵינוּ

shebashoma-yim uvo-oretz.
שֶׁבַּשָּׁמַיִם וּבָאָרֶץ.

one is our God, in heaven and on earth.

■ The six sections of the Mishnah explicate the Written Torah.

SHISHO MI YŌDAY-A.
שִׁשָּׁה מִי יוֹדֵעַ?

Who knows six?

Shisho ani yōday-a.
שִׁשָּׁה אֲנִי יוֹדֵעַ.

I know six;

Shisho sidray mishno.
שִׁשָּׁה סִדְרֵי מִשְׁנָה,

six are the sections of the Mishnah;

Chamisho chum-shay sōro.
חֲמִשָּׁה חֻמְשֵׁי תוֹרָה,

five are the books of the Torah;

Arba imohōs. Sh'lōsho ovōs.
אַרְבַּע אִמָּהוֹת, שְׁלֹשָׁה אָבוֹת,

four are the Matriarchs; three are the Patriarchs;

Sh'nay luchōs hab'ris.
שְׁנֵי לֻחוֹת הַבְּרִית,

two are the tablets of the Covenant;

Echod Elōhaynu
אֶחָד אֱלֹהֵינוּ

shebashoma-yim uvo-oretz.
שֶׁבַּשָּׁמַיִם וּבָאָרֶץ.

one is our God, in heaven and on earth.

■ Even during their period of slavery, they chose the seventh day as their day of rest.

SHIVO MI YŌDAY-A.
שִׁבְעָה מִי יוֹדֵעַ?

Who knows seven?

Shivo ani yōday-a.
שִׁבְעָה אֲנִי יוֹדֵעַ.

I know seven;

Shivo y'may shabato.
שִׁבְעָה יְמֵי שַׁבַּתָּא,

seven are the days of the week;

Shisho sidray mishno.
שִׁשָּׁה סִדְרֵי מִשְׁנָה,

six are the sections of the Mishnah;

Chamisho chum-shay sōro.
חֲמִשָּׁה חֻמְשֵׁי תוֹרָה,

five are the books of the Torah;

nirtzo   halayl   Boraych   tzofun   shulchon ōraych   kōraych   mor

Arba imohōs. Sh'lōsho ovōs.   אַרְבַּע אִמָּהוֹת, שְׁלֹשָׁה אָבוֹת,

four are the Matriarchs; three are the Patriarchs;

Sh'nay luchōs hab'ris.   שְׁנֵי לֻחוֹת הַבְּרִית,

two are the tablets of the Covenant;

Echod Elōhaynu   אֶחָד אֱלֹהֵינוּ

shebashoma-yim uvo-oretz.   שֶׁבַּשָּׁמַיִם וּבָאָרֶץ.

one is our God, in heaven and on earth.

■ Circumcision, usually done on the eighth day of life,
was performed en masse on the eve of the Exodus.

SH'MŌNO MI YŌDAY-A.   שְׁמוֹנָה מִי יוֹדֵעַ?

Who knows eight?

Sh'mōno ani yōday-a.   שְׁמוֹנָה אֲנִי יוֹדֵעַ.

I know eight;

Sh'mōno y'may milo.   שְׁמוֹנָה יְמֵי מִילָה,

eight are the days of circumcision;

Shivo y'may shabato.   שִׁבְעָה יְמֵי שַׁבַּתָּא,

seven are the days of the week;

Shisho sidray mishno.   שִׁשָּׁה סִדְרֵי מִשְׁנָה,

six are the sections of the Mishnah;

Chamisho chum-shay sōro.   חֲמִשָּׁה חֻמְשֵׁי תוֹרָה,

five are the books of the Torah;

Arba imohōs. Sh'lōsho ovōs.   אַרְבַּע אִמָּהוֹת, שְׁלֹשָׁה אָבוֹת,

four are the Matriarchs; three are the Patriarchs;

Sh'nay luchōs hab'ris.   שְׁנֵי לֻחוֹת הַבְּרִית,

two are the tablets of the Covenant;

Echod Elōhaynu   אֶחָד אֱלֹהֵינוּ

shebashoma-yim uvo-oretz.   שֶׁבַּשָּׁמַיִם וּבָאָרֶץ.

one is our God, in heaven and on earth.

■ The Jewish wives were not intimidated by Pharaoh's orders to "cast every son . . .
into the river." Instead, they bore children, placing their trust in God's salvation.

TISHO MI YŌDAY-A.   תִּשְׁעָה מִי יוֹדֵעַ?

Who knows nine?

Tisho ani yōday-a.

תִּשְׁעָה אֲנִי יוֹדֵעַ.

I know nine;

Tisho yarchay laydo.

תִּשְׁעָה יַרְחֵי לֵדָה,

nine are the months of pregnancy;

Sh'mōno y'may milo.

שְׁמוֹנָה יְמֵי מִילָה,

eight are the days of circumcision;

Shivo y'may shabato.

שִׁבְעָה יְמֵי שַׁבַּתָּא,

seven are the days of the week;

Shisho sidray mishno.

שִׁשָּׁה סִדְרֵי מִשְׁנָה,

six are the sections of the Mishnah;

Chamisho chum-shay sōro.

חֲמִשָּׁה חֻמְשֵׁי תוֹרָה,

five are the books of the Torah;

Arba imohōs. Sh'lōsho ovōs.

אַרְבַּע אִמָּהוֹת, שְׁלֹשָׁה אָבוֹת,

four are the Matriarchs; three are the Patriarchs;

Sh'nay luchōs hab'ris.

שְׁנֵי לֻחוֹת הַבְּרִית,

two are the tablets of the Covenant;

Echod Elōhaynu
shebashoma-yim uvo-oretz.

אֶחָד אֱלֹהֵינוּ
שֶׁבַּשָּׁמַיִם וּבָאָרֶץ.

one is our God, in heaven and on earth.

■ The nation would imminently accept the Ten Commandments.

ASORO MI YŌDAY-A.

עֲשָׂרָה מִי יוֹדֵעַ?

Who knows ten?

Asoro ani yōday-a.

עֲשָׂרָה אֲנִי יוֹדֵעַ.

I know ten;

Asoro dib'ra-yo.

עֲשָׂרָה דִבְּרַיָּא,

ten are the Ten Commandments;

Tisho yarchay laydo.

תִּשְׁעָה יַרְחֵי לֵדָה,

nine are the months of pregnancy;

Sh'mōno y'may milo.

שְׁמוֹנָה יְמֵי מִילָה,

eight are the days of circumcision;

Shivo y'may shabato.

שִׁבְעָה יְמֵי שַׁבַּתָּא,

seven are the days of the week;

nirtzo · halayl · Boraych · tzofun · shulchon ōraych · kōraych · morō

Shisho sidray mishno.

שִׁשָּׁה סִדְרֵי מִשְׁנָה,

six are the sections of the Mishnah;

Chamisho chum-shay sōro.

חֲמִשָּׁה חֻמְשֵׁי תוֹרָה,

five are the books of the Torah;

Arba imohōs. Sh'lōsho ovōs.

אַרְבַּע אִמָּהוֹת, שְׁלֹשָׁה אָבוֹת,

four are the Matriarchs; three are the Patriarchs;

Sh'nay luchōs hab'ris.

שְׁנֵי לֻחוֹת הַבְּרִית,

two are the tablets of the Covenant;

Echod Elōhaynu
shebashoma-yim uvo-oretz.

אֶחָד אֱלֹהֵינוּ
שֶׁבַּשָּׁמַיִם וּבָאָרֶץ.

one is our God, in heaven and on earth.

■ The families of Joseph's eleven brothers, represented by the stars in his dream, changed neither their names, language, nor manner of dress in Egypt. (As viceroy, Joseph was given an official name and royal wardrobe by Pharaoh, and spoke the language of the court.)

ACHAD OSOR MI YŌDAY-A.

אַחַד עָשָׂר מִי יוֹדֵעַ?

Who knows eleven?

Achad osor ani yōday-a.

אַחַד עָשָׂר אֲנִי יוֹדֵעַ.

I know eleven;

Achad osor kōch'vayo.

אַחַד עָשָׂר כּוֹכְבַיָּא,

eleven are the stars (constellations);

Asoro dib'ra-yo.

עֲשָׂרָה דִבְּרַיָּא,

ten are the Ten Commandments;

Tisho yarchay laydo.

תִּשְׁעָה יַרְחֵי לֵדָה,

nine are the months of pregnancy;

Sh'mōno y'may milo.

שְׁמוֹנָה יְמֵי מִילָה,

eight are the days of circumcision;

Shivo y'may shabato.

שִׁבְעָה יְמֵי שַׁבַּתָּא,

seven are the days of the week;

Shisho sidray mishno.

שִׁשָּׁה סִדְרֵי מִשְׁנָה,

six are the sections of the Mishnah;

Chamisho chum-shay sōro.

חֲמִשָּׁה חֻמְשֵׁי תוֹרָה,

five are the books of the Torah;

קַדֵּשׁ וּרְחַץ כַּרְפַּס יַחַץ מַגִּיד רָחְצָה מוֹצִיא מַצָּ

atzo   mōtzi   roch'tzo   magid   yachatz   karpas   ur'chatz   kaḋaysh

Arba imohōs. Sh'lōsho ovōs. אַרְבַּע אִמָּהוֹת, שְׁלֹשָׁה אָבוֹת,

four are the Matriarchs; three are the Patriarchs;

Sh'nay luchōs hab'ris. שְׁנֵי לֻחוֹת הַבְּרִית,

two are the tablets of the Covenant;

Echod Elōhaynu אֶחָד אֱלֹהֵינוּ

shebashoma-yim uvo-oretz. שֶׁבַּשָּׁמַיִם וּבָאָרֶץ.

one is our God, in heaven and on earth.

■ All twelve tribes maintained their familial integrity, for no Jewish woman consented to the advances of the Egyptian taskmasters.

SH'NAYM OSOR MI YŌDAY-A. שְׁנֵים עָשָׂר מִי יוֹדֵעַ?

Who knows twelve?

Sh'naym osor ani yōday-a. שְׁנֵים עָשָׂר אֲנִי יוֹדֵעַ.

I know twelve;

Sh'naym osor shivta-yo. שְׁנֵים עָשָׂר שִׁבְטַיָּא,

twelve are the tribes;

Achad osor kōch'va-yo. אַחַד עָשָׂר כּוֹכְבַיָּא,

eleven are the stars;

Asoro dib'ra-yo. עֲשָׂרָה דִבְּרַיָּא,

ten are the Ten Commandments;

Tisho yarchay laydo. תִּשְׁעָה יַרְחֵי לֵדָה,

nine are the months of pregnancy;

Sh'mōno y'may milo. שְׁמוֹנָה יְמֵי מִילָה,

eight are the days of circumcision;

Shivo y'may shabato. שִׁבְעָה יְמֵי שַׁבַּתָּא,

seven are the days of the week;

Shisho sidray mishno. שִׁשָּׁה סִדְרֵי מִשְׁנָה,

six are the sections of the Mishnah;

Chamisho chum-shay sōro. חֲמִשָּׁה חֻמְשֵׁי תוֹרָה,

five are the books of the Torah;

Arba imohōs. Sh'lōsho ovōs. אַרְבַּע אִמָּהוֹת, שְׁלֹשָׁה אָבוֹת,

four are the Matriarchs; three are the Patriarchs;

Sh'nay luchōs hab'ris. שְׁנֵי לֻחוֹת הַבְּרִית,

two are the tablets of the Covenant;

nirtzo · halayl · Borаych · tzofun · shulchon ōraych · kōraych · morо

Echod Elōhaynu
shebashoma-yim uvo-oretz.

אֶחָד אֱלֹהֵינוּ
שֶׁבַּשָּׁמַיִם וּבָאָרֶץ.

one is our God, in heaven and on earth.

■ God taught Moses the prayers of the Thirteen Attributes of Divine Mercy,
to be followed in word and deed, in times of national distress.

SH'LŌSHO OSOR MI YŌDAY-A.   שְׁלֹשָׁה עָשָׂר מִי יוֹדֵעַ?

Who knows thirteen?

Sh'lōsho osor ani yōday-a.

שְׁלֹשָׁה עָשָׂר אֲנִי יוֹדֵעַ.

I know thirteen;

Sh'lōsho osor mida-yo.

שְׁלֹשָׁה עָשָׂר מִדַּיָּא,

thirteen are the attributes of God;

Sh'naym osor shivta-yo.

שְׁנֵים עָשָׂר שִׁבְטַיָּא,

twelve are the tribes;

Achad osor kōch'va-yo.

אַחַד עָשָׂר כּוֹכְבַיָּא,

eleven are the stars (in Joseph's dream);

Asoro dib'ra-yo.

עֲשָׂרָה דִבְּרַיָּא,

ten are the Ten Commandments;

Tisho yarchay laydo.

תִּשְׁעָה יַרְחֵי לֵדָה,

nine are the months of pregnancy;

Sh'mōno y'may milo.

שְׁמוֹנָה יְמֵי מִילָה,

eight are the days of circumcision;

Shivo y'may shabato.

שִׁבְעָה יְמֵי שַׁבַּתָּא,

seven are the days of the week;

Shisho sidray mishno.

שִׁשָּׁה סִדְרֵי מִשְׁנָה,

six are the sections of the Mishnah;

Chamisho chum-shay sōro.

חֲמִשָּׁה חֻמְשֵׁי תוֹרָה,

five are the books of the Torah;

Arba imohōs. Sh'lōsho ovōs.

אַרְבַּע אִמָּהוֹת, שְׁלֹשָׁה אָבוֹת,

four are the Matriarchs; three are the Patriarchs,

Sh'nay luchōs hab'ris.

שְׁנֵי לֻחוֹת הַבְּרִית,

two are the tablets of the Covenant;

Echod Elōhaynu
shebashoma-yim uvo-oretz.

אֶחָד אֱלֹהֵינוּ
שֶׁבַּשָּׁמַיִם וּבָאָרֶץ.

one is our God, in heaven and on earth.

קַדֵּשׁ וּרְחַץ כַּרְפַּס יַחַץ מַגִּיד רָחְצָה מוֹצִיא מַצ

atzo   mōtzi   roch'tzo   magid   yachatz   karpas   ur'chatz   kadaysh

■ Lest one feel, God forbid, that the events of the Exodus are overshadowed by the centuries-long night of the present exile, and seek respite in some lifestyle inconsistent with that prescribed by the Torah, the Haggadah closes with the soliloquy of a lost soul seeking to identify with a higher truth. "The goat supplies my needs — meat, milk, leather, mohair, tent skins — perhaps it is divine! But the cat can easily devour the baby goat — shall I worship the cat? Or the dog that can overpower the cat? . . ." In like fashion, man eliminates worship of brute strength (stick, ox), deification of the elements (fire, water), idolization of man (slaughterer) and adoration of angels. The supremacy of the Holy One, Blessed is He, and the subservience of all of Creation to Him is thus arrived at as the ultimate truth.

CHAD GADYO. Chad gadyo,   חַד גַּדְיָא, חַד גַּדְיָא,
A kid, a kid,

d'zabin abo bisray zuzay.   דְּזַבִּין אַבָּא בִּתְרֵי זוּזֵי,
that father bought for two zuzim,

Chad gadyo, chad gadyo.   חַד גַּדְיָא חַד גַּדְיָא.
a kid, a kid.

V'oso shun'ro, v'och'lo l'gadyo,   וְאָתָא שׁוּנְרָא וְאָכְלָה לְגַדְיָא,
Then came the cat and devoured the kid,

d'zabin abo bisray zuzay.   דְּזַבִּין אַבָּא בִּתְרֵי זוּזֵי,
that father bought for two zuzim,

Chad gadyo, chad gadyo.   חַד גַּדְיָא חַד גַּדְיָא.
a kid, a kid.

V'oso chalbo, v'noshach l'shun'ro,   וְאָתָא כַלְבָּא וְנָשַׁךְ לְשׁוּנְרָא,
Then came the dog, which bit the cat,

d'och'lo l'gadyo,   דְּאָכְלָא לְגַדְיָא,
which devoured the kid,

d'zabin abo bisray zuzay.   דְּזַבִּין אַבָּא בִּתְרֵי זוּזֵי,
that father bought for two zuzim,

Chad gadyo, chad gadyo.   חַד גַּדְיָא חַד גַּדְיָא.
a kid, a kid,

V'oso chut'ro, v'hiko l'chalbo,   וְאָתָא חוּטְרָא וְהִכָּה לְכַלְבָּא,
Then came the stick, and beat the dog,

d'noshach l'shun'ro,   דְּנָשַׁךְ לְשׁוּנְרָא,
that bit the cat,

d'och'lo l'gadyo,   דְּאָכְלָה לְגַדְיָא,
that devoured the kid,

 נ׳רְצה halayl Boraych tzofun shulchon öraych köraych moro

דְּזַבִּין אַבָּא בִּתְרֵי זוּזֵי,

d'zabin abo bisray zuzay.

that father bought for two zuzim,

חַד גַּדְיָא חַד גַּדְיָא.

Chad gadyo, chad gadyo.

a kid, a kid.

וְאָתָא **נוּרָא** וְשָׂרַף לְחוּטְרָא,

V'oso nuro, v'soraf l'chutro,

Then came fire, and burnt the stick,

דְּהִכָּה לְכַלְבָּא,

d'hiko l'chalbo.

that beat the dog,

דְּנָשַׁךְ לְשׁוּנְרָא,

d'noshach l'shunro,

that bit the cat,

דְּאָכְלָה לְגַדְיָא,

d'och'lo l'gadyo,

that devoured the kid

דְּזַבִּין אַבָּא בִּתְרֵי זוּזֵי,

d'zabin abo bisray zuzay.

that father bought for two zuzim,

חַד גַּדְיָא חַד גַּדְיָא.

Chad gadyo, chad gadyo.

a kid, a kid.

וְאָתָא **מַיָּא** וְכָבָה לְנוּרָא,

V'oso ma-yo, v'chovo l'nuro,

Then came water, and quenched the fire,

דְּשָׂרַף לְחוּטְרָא,

d'soraf l'chut'ro,

that burnt the stick,

דְּהִכָּה לְכַלְבָּא,

d'hiko l'chalbo,

that beat the dog,

דְּנָשַׁךְ לְשׁוּנְרָא,

d'noshach l'shun'ro,

that bit the cat,

דְּאָכְלָה לְגַדְיָא,

d'och'lo l'gadyo,

that devoured the kid

דְּזַבִּין אַבָּא בִּתְרֵי זוּזֵי,

d'zabin abo bisray zuzay.

that father bought for two zuzim,

חַד גַּדְיָא חַד גַּדְיָא.

Chad gadyo, chad gadyo.

a kid, a kid.

וְאָתָא **תוֹרָא** וְשָׁתָה לְמַיָּא,

V'oso sōro v'shoso l'ma-yo,

Then came the ox, and drank the water,

דְּכָבָה לְנוּרָא,

d'chovo l'nuro,

that quenched the fire,

d'soraf l'chutro,   דְּשָׂרַף לְחוּטְרָא,
that burnt the stick,

d'hiko l'chalbo,   דְּהִכָּה לְכַלְבָּא,
that beat the dog,

d'noshach l'shun'ro,   דְּנָשַׁךְ לְשׁוּנְרָא,
that bit the cat,

d'och'lo l'gadyo.   דְּאָכְלָה לְגַדְיָא,
that devoured the kid

d'zabin abo bisray zuzay.   דְּזַבִּין אַבָּא בִּתְרֵי זוּזֵי,
that father bought for two zuzim,

Chad gadyo, chad gadyo.   חַד גַּדְיָא חַד גַּדְיָא.
a kid, a kid.

V'oso hashōchayt   **וְאָתָא הַשּׁוֹחֵט**
  v'shochat l'sōro,   וְשָׁחַט לְתוֹרָא,
Then came the slaughterer, and slaughtered the ox,

d'shoso l'ma-yo,   דְּשָׁתָא לְמַיָּא,
that drank the water,

d'chovo l'nuro,   דְּכָבָה לְנוּרָא,
that quenched the fire,

d'soraf l'chutro,   דְּשָׂרַף לְחוּטְרָא,
that burnt the stick,

d'hiko l'chalbo,   דְּהִכָּה לְכַלְבָּא,
that beat the dog,

d'noshach l'shun'ro,   דְּנָשַׁךְ לְשׁוּנְרָא,
that bit the cat,

d'och'lo l'gadyo,   דְּאָכְלָה לְגַדְיָא,
that devoured the kid

d'zabin abo bisray zuzay.   דְּזַבִּין אַבָּא בִּתְרֵי זוּזֵי,
that father bought for two zuzim,

Chad gadyo, chad gadyo.   חַד גַּדְיָא חַד גַּדְיָא.
a kid, a kid.

V'oso malach hamo-ves,   **וְאָתָא מַלְאַךְ הַמָּוֶת**
  v'shochat l'shōchayt,   וְשָׁחַט לְשׁוֹחֵט,
Then came the angel of death, and killed the slaughterer,

d'shochat l'sōro,	דְּשָׁחַט לְתוֹרָא,
who slaughtered the ox,	
d'shoso l'ma-yo.	דְּשָׁתָה לְמַיָּא,
that drank the water,	
d'chovo l'nuro,	דְּכָבָה לְנוּרָא,
that quenched the fire,	
d'soraf l'chutro,	דְּשָׂרַף לְחוּטְרָא,
that burnt the stick,	
d'hiko l'chalbo,	דְּהִכָּה לְכַלְבָּא,
that beat the dog,	
d'noshach l'shunro,	דְּנָשַׁךְ לְשׁוּנְרָא,
that bit the cat,	
d'och'lo l'gadyo,	דְּאָכְלָה לְגַדְיָא,
that devoured the kid	
d'zabin abo bisray zuzay.	דְּזַבִּין אַבָּא בִּתְרֵי זוּזֵי,
that father bought for two zuzim,	
Chad gadyo, chad gadyo.	חַד גַּדְיָא חַד גַּדְיָא.
a kid, a kid.	
V'oso Hakodōsh boruch hu	**וְאָתָא הַקָּדוֹשׁ בָּרוּךְ הוּא**
Then came the Holy One, Blessed is He,	
v'shochat l'malach hamo-ves,	וְשָׁחַט לְמַלְאַךְ הַמָּוֶת,
and slew the angel of death,	
d'shochat l'shōchayt,	דְּשָׁחַט לְשׁוֹחֵט,
who killed the slaughterer,	
d'shochat l'sōro,	דְּשָׁחַט לְתוֹרָא,
who slaughtered the ox,	
d'shoso l'ma-yo.	דְּשָׁתָה לְמַיָּא,
that drank the water,	
d'chovo l'nuro,	דְּכָבָה לְנוּרָא,
that quenched the fire,	
d'soraf l'chutro,	דְּשָׂרַף לְחוּטְרָא,
that burnt the stick,	
d'hiko l'chalbo,	דְּהִכָּה לְכַלְבָּא,
that beat the dog,	

atzo mōtzi roch'tzo magīd yachatz karpas ur'chatz kadaysh קַדֵּשׁ וּרְחַץ כַּרְפַּס יַחַץ מַגִּיד רַחְצָה מוֹצִיא מַצָּ

d'noshach l'shunro,

that bit the cat,

דְּנָשַׁךְ לְשׁוּנְרָא,

d'och'lo l'gadyo,

that devoured the kid

דְּאָכְלָה לְגַדְיָא,

d'zabin abo bisray zuzay.

that father bought for two zuzim,

דְּזַבִּין אַבָּא בִּתְרֵי זוּזֵי,

Chad gadyo, chad gadyo.

a kid, a kid.

חַד גַּדְיָא חַד גַּדְיָא.

ALTHOUGH THE HAGGADAH FORMALLY ENDS AT THIS POINT, ONE SHOULD CONTINUE TO OCCUPY HIMSELF WITH THE STORY OF THE EXODUS, AND THE LAWS OF PASSOVER, UNTIL SLEEP OVERTAKES HIM. MANY RECITE *SONG OF SONGS* AFTER THE HAGGADAH.

This volume is part of
THE ARTSCROLL SERIES®
an ongoing project of
translations, commentaries and expositions
on Scripture, Mishnah, Talmud, Halachah,
liturgy, history, the classic Rabbinic writings,
biographies and thought.

For a brochure of current publications
visit your local Hebrew bookseller
or contact the publisher:

Mesorah Publications, ltd

4401 Second Avenue
Brooklyn, New York 11232
(718) 921-9000
www.artscroll.com